# Work Goes Mobile

## Nokia's Lessons from the Leading Edge

Michael Lattanzi
Antti Korhonen
Vishy Gopalakrishnan

John Wiley & Sons, Ltd

Published 2006 by     John Wiley & Sons Ltd, The Atrium, Southern Gate, Chichester,
West Sussex PO19 8SQ, England

Telephone   (+44) 1243 779777

Email (for orders and customer service enquiries): cs-books@wiley.co.uk
Visit our Home Page on www.wiley.com

Other Wiley Editorial Offices

John Wiley & Sons Inc., 111 River Street, Hoboken, NJ 07030, USA

Jossey-Bass, 989 Market Street, San Francisco, CA 94103-1741, USA

Wiley-VCH Verlag GmbH, Boschstr. 12, D-69469 Weinheim, Germany

John Wiley & Sons Australia Ltd, 42 McDougall Street, Milton, Queensland 4064, Australia

John Wiley & Sons (Asia) Pte Ltd, 2 Clementi Loop #02-01, Jin Xing Distripark, Singapore 129809

John Wiley & Sons Canada Ltd, 22 Worcester Road, Etobicoke, Ontario, Canada M9W 1L1

Wiley also publishes its books in a variety of electronic formats. Some content that appears in print may
not be available in electronic books.

British Library Cataloguing in Publication Data

A catalogue record for this book is available from the British Library

ISBN 13 978-0-470-02752-3 (HB)
ISBN 10 0-470-02752-5 (HB)

Typeset in Zaph Humanist 11 pt by DataClub, Helsinki, Finland
Printed and bound in Great Britain by TJ International Ltd, Padstow, Cornwall, UK
This book is printed on acid-free paper responsibly manufactured from sustainable forestry
in which at least two trees are planted for each one used for paper production.

# Contents

# Foreword

Business mobility—what was once considered a corner-office perk is steadily becoming mainstream. As businesses begin to realize the advantages of making quality information available to workers while they are on the move, more employees—in-house and field-based, in all functions and at all levels—are beginning to consider this "perk" a vital part of successfully doing business.

While mobile email is probably the most prevalent example of business mobility today, only a small percentage of the total number of corporate email boxes have been mobilized. The worldwide potential for freeing more workers from their desks over the next few years by using mobile email technologies is staggering.

And email is not the only thing happening in the world of mobile business. Fixed-to-Mobile Convergence (FMC) voice solutions based on open industry standards are making inroads on corporate telecommunications budgets. These solutions allow companies to equip employees with a single communication device that roams as needed between the corporate network and external carrier networks—eliminating the need for a mobile number and an office number.

While the benefits of mobility are plenty, transforming to new ways of working that are free from traditional constraints of geography is the hard part. In fact, companies seeking to implement systems and processes that provide quality information to their workers wherever they are face a laundry list of challenges. Security, cost, technological adaptability, training, and the internal process of accepting and effectively using mobility often complicate matters. In the face of these challenges, it is no wonder that society is just beginning to evolve toward mobility as the way of doing business.

Helping businesses understand mobility, its challenges, and ways to manage those challenges are at the core of this book. At Nokia, we believe that our hands-on, real-life experience provides a trusted guide for business decision makers weighing the challenges and advantages of mobilizing their workforce. *Work Goes Mobile* is intended to help you 1) answer fundamental questions about how mobility can benefit your organization, and 2) decide on the best course of action to untether your business activities from specific places and times.

I've always believed that smart companies do as they say. This gives them two powerful advantages: insight and credibility. Insight comes as the company experiences what its customers live every day. Confronting those same challenges lets the company focus on improvements that directly solve customer pain points. Credibility grows as customers see that the company has faith in its products and services, relying on them as an integral part of its business infrastructure.

Nokia claims leadership in mobility because we are committed to mobilizing our own business. We have done our homework, carried out our due diligence, and are successfully using mobile capabilities to gain significant business advantages. *Work Goes Mobile* is Nokia's contribution to the growth and acceptance of having easy access to real-time, quality information while on the move as a fundamental part of doing business.

If you can identify compelling reasons to begin moving your organization toward mobility, this can be a useful guide. If you allow us to, Nokia can help your organization begin enjoying the freedom and benefits of business mobility.

Mary McDowell
Executive VP and General Manager
Nokia Enterprise Solutions
New York

# Acknowledgements

Without the ongoing efforts of Nokia employees worldwide, we would have had very little to write about. Our goal has been to capture their experience and organize it into a useful tool for people interested in seeing what mobility can do for their business. To accomplish that end, we called on the skills, knowledge, enthusiasm, patience, and good humor of many people, and we want to publicly thank them.

First, heartfelt thanks go to our families: Michael—Connie, Rachel, Alyssa, and Jonathan; Antti—Merja, Helmi, and Oskar; Vishy—Geetha, Gautam, and Ashwin. For many months, they endured our long workdays and phone calls at odd hours. Without their unstinting support, encouragement, and patience, we could never have finished this book.

We want to thank Jonathan Fischer for stepping in during the development process to provide a great deal of information on mobile technology. Because of his subject matter expertise and his never-give-up attitude, the chapter on mobile technology enablers is much more complete.

We are also deeply grateful to Aki Laiho, Bethany Davis, and Lucy Hur for being so generous with their time. In spite of their demanding day jobs, they read the entire manuscript with a keen eye for accuracy, clarity, and structure. Their unique insight and expertise significantly enhanced the quality of this book.

While mobility is a corporate-wide initiative involving hundreds of people at Nokia, a core group of supporters who believed in the value of sharing Nokia's experience contributed significantly to this book: Ari Hakkarainen, Collin Hayes, Jyrki Kivimäki, Miika Kuha, Megan Matthews, Veli-Matti Pelho, Matti Pylkkänen, and Outi Vuorio. Their coaching and suggestions went a long way toward making this project a success.

Next, we would like to recognize Jennifer Rey, Scott Hatch, Robbi Killpack, and Lyn Worthen for calmly reviewing and editing endless drafts of our chapters. Their careful suggestions helped this book take shape and eventually come alive. We also thank the team at DataClub who handled the pre-press process and all of the folks at Wiley who walked us through the publication and final production processes.

Many thanks also go to Mary McDowell, Mikko Kosonen, Tero Ojanperä, John Robinson, and Jyrki Rosenberg, all members of our Executive Advisory Committee. They provided strong support and encouragement throughout the project.

Last, but certainly not least, we would like to give special recognition to JP Finnell for his unwavering dedication and leadership throughout this endeavor. Without his energy and focus on overcoming some tough challenges, this book would never have become a reality. Thanks again, JP!

# Introduction

*Should we go mobile?* That was the question Nokia senior executives were debating in early 2002. Like most organizations, Nokia was searching for ways to cut costs as they rode out the market slump of the early 2000s. Investing precious time and resources in a broad, complicated concept such as mobility might seem like a risky path to take in tough market conditions, but Nokia was determined to understand and realize the potential benefits that providing right-time, quality information to workers on the move could bring to its business.

Simply hearing the word *Nokia* evokes images of freedom of movement, of staying connected wherever you are; after all, Nokia is the world's most recognized mobile phone and mobile technology brand. Its corporate mission—to be a leading example of connecting people—underscored the need to demonstrate the organization's commitment to improving mobile access to critical business information and processes, even in difficult economic times.

Behind closed doors, executives debated tough questions:

- What does it mean to mobilize our business?

- Can portability of and reliable access to information really reduce costs and increase productivity?

- How will flexible working times and places affect management practices?

- Should we take this path?

These and many others all boiled down to one simple question: *Can you mobilize a business and gain significant business benefits from it?*

The answer lies here, in this book. *Work Goes Mobile: Nokia's Lessons from the Leading Edge* is a case study and methodology for business decision makers who want to understand and guide their organization through the next natural transformation in the way they do business. It is not meant to provide a definitive analysis of mobility tools and technologies, but rather a starting point for planning how to mobilize a business. The perspective is that of a large, global company, but the knowledge and concepts presented here apply to businesses of many sizes.

As you read through this book you will discover, as Nokia did, that

- Mobility is a business solution that solves real business problems and provides real business benefits.

- Mobility is a fundamental change in the way we work.

- Mobility is more than just technology.

- Mobility is best approached as evolution—not revolution.

Identifying and clearly defining mobile solutions that simplify business communication and activity is not a simple task. Authors Michael Lattanzi, Antti Korhonen, and Vishy Gopalakrishnan know this all too well—they've been through the process at Nokia and with its customers. In *Work Goes Mobile* they call on their experiences to help you to achieve the following:

- Understand what mobility really means by examining what a mobilized business is and by discussing the challenges and benefits associated with this new way of working.

- Prepare your organization's people, processes, and technologies for the transition to working in more flexible and efficient ways.

- Gain the knowledge, tools, and guidance you need to develop solid, compelling business cases for mobility solutions.

The knowledge presented in this book results from a careful analysis of Nokia's experience from 2001 to 2005—its approach, struggles, and discoveries along the evolutionary path toward mobility. The authors explain that putting information at people's fingertips—regardless of their location or the time of day—is a complex process that should be viewed and approached from various perspectives.

The authors emphasize that Nokia's most successful approach to achieving this vision began by understanding user needs and by examining business processes. The company then proceeded to choosing the right tools, technologies, and infrastructure, while at the same time focusing on modifying real estate and facilities to support new places of work. Most importantly, the authors point out that Nokia is still discovering and implementing mobility solutions that make doing business easier.

Business mobility is on the rise—now is the time for decision makers to examine how the convenience and flexibility of having access to the right information at the right time can produce compelling, tangible business benefits. Let Nokia's experience help you prepare your business to thrive in this emerging mobile environment.

# I

# Understanding Mobility

# 1

# The Nokia Journey

*At first, we just wanted to showcase mobility. We did not have any grand notions of fundamentally changing the way we work at Nokia. But, we learned the hard way that you really do need a clear, long-term goal of mobilizing everything that makes sense. Once you set that goal, it is easier to draft a high-level master plan and roadmap, followed by implementing based on the business case for each component. Now that we have actually taken the first steps, it looks like we are on the right track—we are starting to see the benefits of mobility, and our master plan is giving us the clear direction we need.*

*—Mikko Kosonen, CIO and Senior VP*
*Nokia Business Infrastructure*

# An Unhappy CIO

"I don't believe you." Stunned silence followed this comment, made by the CIO in a conference room at Nokia's headquarters in Espoo, Finland. "We are Nokia, the mobility company. Yet you tell me that connecting people is not something we can do internally, even though we tell millions of people every day that we can and do?" Such was the CIO's reaction when an information technology task force reported on opportunities to mobilize applications, systems, and processes at Nokia in mid-2002.

"No, no…nothing like that. Our study simply indicates that only a small percentage of our internal applications and processes would realize cost savings by adding mobility."

"Well, I have seen your report. But I refuse to believe that we cannot improve our performance by mobilizing a much larger percentage of our IT infrastructure. For example, the facilities team is mobilizing our workforce by using flexible space; they are cutting costs and improving productivity. And they are implementing Nokia's vision of being a leading example of connecting people via mobility. It can be done."

Fortunately for Nokia (and for the rest of this book), someone in that meeting took the unhappy CIO's comments to heart and started a low-profile study to identify the opportunities that supposedly did not exist.

## A Different Perspective

The low-profile study produced very different results from the first report. The study's project team identified many potential opportunities, finding that a large percentage of Nokia's existing systems, processes, and applications were good candidates for some level of mobilization. Why the marked difference in findings? It boiled down to point of view. Cost savings drove the findings of the IT task force report, while user adoption and productivity improvements were the deciding factors in what made the low-profile study's opportunity list. On the basis of this and earlier studies, the company began its journey toward mobility as a way of business.

# Starting Down the Path

In early 2003, Nokia had several groups exploring and deploying mobility technologies, with a lot of smart people working on the best ways to provide right-time, quality information to Nokia's workforce regardless of location or the time of day. While the groups were aware of each other's existence, differing management perspectives about primary focus areas kept them from collaborating for almost a year.

The fact was that business mobility was incredibly complex and unexamined below the surface. Even though the groups were charting the same territory, their focus differed—one concentrated on cost savings while the other focused on user adoption and productivity. This decentralization led to a certain amount of disorder:

- Duplication of effort

- Insufficient cost control and accountability

- Regional differences in focus area and development priorities

- Diverging adoption of proprietary and open solutions and platforms

Finally, some frustrated members of each group managed to cut through the confusion and convince their management that mobility was larger than their individual projects. At about the same time, Nokia established a global business group called Enterprise Solutions, which provided a catalyst for speeding up mobility discussions, planning, and change programs.

In late 2003, members of these groups met to discuss their projects. Mobility by this time was a common term at Nokia, but with somewhat overlapping definitions. After lengthy discussions about mobility from each group's perspective, a newly fused group—referred to in this book as the mobility team—was proposed and approved. The team developed a holistic plan to mobilize Nokia's business focused around the following six actions:

1. Conduct an inventory of current mobility-related initiatives.

2. Understand divergent approaches and development priorities.

3. Organize a centralized program management function with cross-unit authority.

4. Identify key focus areas and build internal funding support.

5. Create a strategic roadmap to guide development priorities and requirements.

6. Establish a master plan for implementing mobility solutions, measuring progress, and harvesting lessons learned.

# Why Mobilize Your Business?

One critical outcome of Nokia's drive toward mobile ways of working has been a refined answer to the question "Why mobilize?" Mobility offers the following advantages:

- It makes organizations more agile and quicker to respond to change.

- It accelerates naturally mobile processes such as customer and field service.

- It shortens the cycle time of many conventional business processes through automated alerts and other functions.

- It changes typical slack time into productive time.

- It provides a good opportunity to reduce costs and in some cases to eliminate dependency on existing legacy systems.

- It encourages diversity in work practices by offering freedom of choice about how, where, and when to work.

- It promotes virtual organizational models.

- It supports a healthy balance between work and personal life.

And, obviously for Nokia, developing innovative mobile technology and capabilities promotes practical use of mobility in everyday work.

As with most complex undertakings, Nokia's mobility journey has been complicated and fraught with obstacles, such as the following:

- Dealing with maturing technologies
- Coping with the lack of empirical data on large-scale transformations
- Justifying benefits that are difficult to articulate
- Handling people management changes
- Designing ways to optimize mobile workplaces

And that journey is still far from over. However, in spite of the difficulties, we believe that we have made good progress. Where we are now is the result of excellent effort at all levels of the company. And where we are going is a direct result of the ground our employees are covering right now.

> Increasingly, business happens outside the conventional boundaries of a location. Mobility is about providing information at the point of business.

Even as we share our experience here, hoping to help other businesses avoid many of the obstacles we have faced, Nokia continues to forge ahead on the road toward mobility as a way of doing business. The following chapters expand the story presented here, providing the background, understanding, and tools needed to successfully assess an organization's mobility needs and prepare a holistic approach to creating new ways of working that transcend traditional working times and places.

## Things to Consider

- Nokia is committed to developing and implementing solutions that deliver right-time, quality information to workers while they are on the move. Does taking a similar stance make sense for your organization?

- By looking for ways to accelerate naturally mobile processes like customer service, you can help your organization become more agile and quicker to respond to change. What processes in your organization are naturally mobile?

- Think about your own organization. Are there competing or uncoordinated mobility initiatives in progress? How could your organization benefit from bringing them together?

# 2

# What Is a Mobilized Business?

*A mobilized business operates at the full potential of its people.*
*It allows you to tap into talent and capabilities—no matter where*
*they are. It unleashes your people, letting them be flexible and*
*responsive to the demands of your business.*

—Mary McDowell, Executive VP and General Manager
Nokia Enterprise Solutions

Mobility. The word has been around for the past few years, typically used in connection with cellular or mobile phones, and more recently with mobile email. But when it comes right down to it, what does mobility mean?

Ask ten people for a definition of mobility, and the majority will mention "freedom of movement." Mobility is the freedom to collaborate and transact business outside traditional work places and times. The overwhelming use of mobile phones and other wireless devices indicates that today—more than ever—workers are staying connected while they are on the go.

Consider this scenario: Your client, located three time zones earlier than you, contacts you at the beginning of their business day with an urgent request for the latest technical details and pricing on your product. Their corporate purchasing group is going to make the buy/no-buy decision at the end of their business day. You have been trying to close this account for months. But, it is 8:00 pm in your time zone, and you are at your daughter's last concert of the season. The information you need is at the office, over 30 minutes away.

Will you have to miss your daughter's concert to take care of this important business activity? Not if you work for a mobilized business.

You grab your mobile device, access the corporate network, pull the latest technical and pricing data from the product database, and email the information to your client. You call the client to let them know they will have the details in their inbox in a few minutes and wish them well in the meeting. And you return to enjoying your daughter's concert.

# Perspectives on Mobility

Ask a CEO what mobility is, and she may say that it is the ability to respond to pending emails while on the way to the airport. For sales representatives, it is the ability to access important information while visiting customers. For a knowledge worker on a virtual team, it is the ability to make it to his son's basketball game at 4:00 pm but still receive and review that important document by the end of the workday. Mobility enhances productivity by adding flexibility to traditional work routines so that they can be done at the right time regardless of location. Essentially, mobility makes it easier to manage the complicated and ever-increasing demands of both work and personal life.

Mobility means different things to different people. Like the group of blind people, each touching a different part of the elephant and interpreting it as a rope, a tree trunk, a pot, a basket, a plowshare, and so on, each person in an organization will form an opinion of mobility based on his or her predominant perspective. It takes careful planning, investigation, and communication to help all the functions see and understand the whole mobility elephant.

## What Mobility Is Not

When the talk turns to mobility, some false assumptions tend to surface. One notion claims that mobile workers are not as available as their office counterparts. But technology enables mobile workers in the same way it enables office workers. Mobile workers have access to teleconferences, net meetings, conference calls, and contact through their mobile devices, so they can participate equally in business and decision-making processes.

At Nokia, the use of teleconferences and online meeting tools has grown dramatically. In 2002, Nokia employees clocked an average of one million teleconference minutes per month. In mid-2005, that number had increased to eight million conference minutes per month, resulting in reduced travel time and costs as well as increased involvement in decision making.

> In a mobile business, you are free to work where, when, and how it makes sense.

But lack of availability is only one of many often incorrect assumptions about the use of mobility in business practices. The following table presents comments typically heard when people start talking about a mobilized business.

| Comment | Assumption | Reality |
|---|---|---|
| Your company is mobile? You must use a lot of independent contractors and home office workers. | The workforce is composed of a loose or virtual collection of self-interested workers. | Mobility allows greater access to people with the right skills to solve a business problem—no matter where they are located. |
| My department decided to get everyone these fancy phones that can access the customer support database from anywhere in the region. They're trying to suck every minute they can out of us! | Management thinks their workers are not working hard enough and do not manage their work time well enough. | Mobility is not intended to increase workloads; it helps a worker become more efficient and productive with the time they have dedicated to work. |
| Now that my boss can reach me anytime, does that mean I'll always have to answer his calls—even if it's late at night? | Workers will have to be available to work anytime... the line between work and personal life is gone. | Mobility does not extend the work day—it provides greater ability to flex work time around a worker's personal schedule while maintaining the worker's productivity. |
| How will we be able to build relationships or get to know our colleagues if nobody is in the same place? | Relationships cannot be built unless people are face to face. | Mobility can increase the ability to build relationships by providing a means to initiate and maintain communication and information exchange at a moment's notice, even when the workforce is separated. |

Mobility in and of itself is neither positive nor negative. Rather, it represents a fundamental shift in the way we look at work and doing business. People's attitudes and assumptions are largely determined by the way mobility is presented to them.

## Nokia's Perspective on Mobility

At Nokia, we see mobility as the next step in the natural evolution of doing business. Figure 1 illustrates the evolutionary path that Nokia's business infrastructure has taken over the last 10 years.

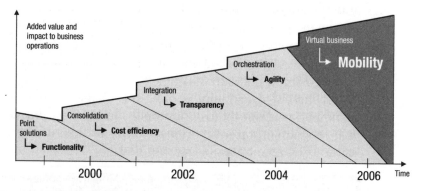

Figure 1. Mobility is the next step in business infrastructure evolution.

As with many other organizations, in the mid-1990s Nokia's infrastructure was a loose collection of *point solutions* that supported individual business units. For example, almost every business had its own email and ERP systems, as well as its own IT organization. With cost efficiency in systems driving our efforts, we *consolidated* our application and IT development into one internal service provider organization that cooperated closely with different business units. Around the same time, Nokia experienced a logistics crisis, which prompted us to begin developing a corporate-wide SAP implementation that would replace all existing ERP systems. Most of Nokia's current global system platforms were created during this consolidation phase.

In the early 2000s, we began concentrating on internal and external *integration* as a means to transparently manage our business throughout the value chain. During this phase, we realized the importance of developing new business capabilities through concurrent IT and process engineering. To accomplish this, we expanded the scope of our IT organization to include business process development, thus consolidating process and system development. We also pursued e-business integration with our customers' and suppliers' systems, resulting in RosettaNet, Nokia's solution to exposing appropriate online systems to its external partners.

Starting in 2003, Nokia began an evolutionary phase called *orchestration*. The main driver for this phase was agility in adapting to change. In this phase, Nokia invested heavily in modularizing processes and platforms, with the goal of staying competitive and productive while adapting to new situations. Internally, this investment improved our capability to reorganize quickly if Nokia decided to fundamentally change its business structure to adapt to changing market directions. Externally, we focused on selecting the best partners to work with to quickly adapt to changing market conditions.

Nokia sees mobility as the key driver for *virtual business*, the next evolutionary phase in business infrastructure. We strongly believe that new ways of working that are free from traditional constraints of geography and time will play an important role in further enhancing our productivity and competitiveness by enabling a virtual business environment.

> Mobility is communication on the go, with access to the right information at the right time.

While each company's experience is unique, most companies have walked some part of this evolutionary path. Anyone who has been in business for the last 10 to 15 years can attest to the forces that have driven companies along this path. In terms of technology, the following transitions have influenced strategic infrastructure decisions:

- Paper to digital vehicles in business processes

- Proprietary to standards-based applications

- Proprietary, closed network architectures to open, IP-based connectivity

Additionally, and just as importantly, changing perspectives on how business is done are rapidly eroding traditional concepts of work, as illustrated in the following table.

| Concept | Traditional view | Emerging view |
|---|---|---|
| Where work takes place | The office | Where it makes most sense |
| How performance is measured | Hours logged | Results achieved |
| How teams collaborate | Permanent physical location<br>Entire team in one location | Virtual spaces<br>Temporary physical locations across geographies |
| Space and facility requirements | A cube for each worker | Flexible meeting and work spaces |
| Organizational models | Strict departmental hierarchies | Worldwide virtual teams that form as needed to address specific initiatives |

# Evolving Toward a Mobilized Business

Changes in working patterns and behaviors fostered by mobile voice—getting access to the right people when they are needed—are strong indicators that the shift to mobile business practices is already underway. Increased offerings of mobile data services are furthering this trend:

- Many businesses have become *laptop mobile*, freeing their workers from their desks.

- The growth of wireless access is rapidly increasing workers' ability to access company information anywhere.

- Upcoming higher bandwidth and capacity in mobile data services will accelerate demand for access to richer information and will amplify the need to change existing business practices.

Obviously, mobile ways of working are quickly becoming a reality. But what are the key changes that mobility brings to work? Mobility enhances business-wide processes and infrastructure, enabling workers to move freely yet sustain and/or increase their productivity (see Figure 2 below):

- Location and time of day are no longer obstacles to doing business.

- Information input and output are possible regardless of the device that employees use to access it.

- Access to information, whether online (wireless) or offline (synchronized copies), is available as needed.

In short, mobility means that business processes, infrastructure, and culture all support flexible and efficient ways of getting the job done.

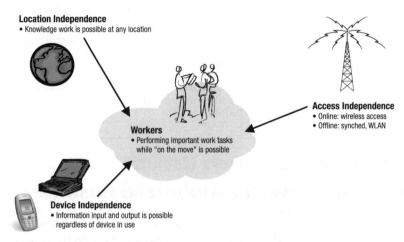

Figure 2. Mobility means access, device, and location independence.

## How Mobility Changes Traditional Business

The overriding effect of mobility on traditional business practices is that it removes location from the process of delivering critical, relevant information to workers. At Nokia, we are finding that increasing a worker's mobility triggers a gradual shift away from traditional work practices:

- Working physically in the office during set daily hours will shift to working wherever and whenever needed.

- Traditional performance measurement based on supervised presence will change to dynamic, task-based measurement.

- Direct supervision will evolve into mentoring, coaching, and connecting people.

- Establishing teams in the same physical location will move toward orchestrating virtual groups of specialized individuals.

- Allocating office space based on status and corporate hierarchy will move toward allocating space to facilitate functions and tasks.

In addition, mobility has the potential to trigger advances in other technologies. And, by its very nature, it will reinforce current trends in organizations to move away from rigid, centralized hierarchies to looser groups that rely on inexpensive, ubiquitous connectivity to get things done. With these thoughts in mind, we share Nokia's insight into how mobility will increasingly change traditional business in the following ways:

- The way we work

- The way we value work

- The way we manage work

## Trends Toward Business Mobility

Mobility is already a part of doing business today, and its role will only become stronger. The most prevalent example today is mobile email. While a relatively small slice of the current business mobility market, mobile email is on the verge of significant growth—perhaps even becoming a mass-market commodity for organizations around the globe over the next few years. In fact, it is estimated that there are currently 650 million corporate email boxes worldwide, but only a fraction of those have been mobilized. Just as email transformed how we do business, the use of mobile email, paired with access to calendar information, corporate networks, and the internet, will free workers from the need to be in a certain location to get their jobs done.

New mobile business solutions like Fixed-to-Mobile Convergence (FMC) voice solutions are also becoming more popular. These solutions integrate mobile and fixed-line networks (the corporate desk phone), providing enterprise telephony services to mobile workers regardless of their location, access technology, and communication device. Essentially, FMC removes the need for an office phone number because the worker's mobile device can receive calls wherever the worker is, with the call being routed over the most cost-effective network (corporate when in the office; external when out and about).

These two examples, out of many others, illustrate that the emphasis on work is shifting from a specific place or time to having access to the right people and information at the right time. Where you are is not so important as who or what you can access.

### The Way We Work

Mobility changes the way we get our work done by affecting traditional concepts of place, time, interaction, information, and technology. Essentially, mobility enables pervasive connectivity, which opens up new work patterns for accessing, processing, and exchanging information. The consequences of pervasive connectivity and easy access to information include the following:

- Separating place from information in business practices and processes (the ability to work almost anywhere)
- Changing the concept of work from hours spent in the office to tasks performed to keep the business working efficiently
- Changing the role of physical corporate facilities to support work wherever it takes place
- Increasing time spent working in virtual, global teams that are formed as needed
- Increasing reliance on virtual collaboration infrastructures
- Increasing accountability for decision making through immediate access to quality information
- Accelerating the flow of information in business processes
- Placing higher burdens on technology infrastructures

### The Way We Value Work

Mobility also changes the value that we place on work by focusing on the relevance of workers' knowledge and the contribution of their activities to meeting business goals:

- The value of work will shift from the place of work to the knowledge of the worker.
- Workers will concentrate on high value-adding tasks that quantifiably and positively affect the business.
- People will be able to work collaboratively or individually in environments that stimulate their creativity.
- Productivity expectations for traditional downtime (commuting, traveling, working off-site, and so on) will increase.
- Team dynamics will be based on high individual performance, and the role of virtual teams will increase with the emphasis on task achievement.

### The Way We Manage Work

One of the greatest impacts mobility will have on traditional business practices is in workforce management:

- As the workforce becomes more mobile and physical presence is removed from the work equation, direct supervision of employees will diminish.

- Work tasks and performance measures will need to be clearly defined as the amount of physical interaction between managers and workers decreases.

- Businesses will need to emphasize personal accountability and individual decision making because mobile workers will decide how, when, and where they complete their tasks.

- Managers and employees will need to develop stronger relationships of trust to maintain productive work environments.

- As teams become more mobile and virtual, management responsibilities will focus on connecting people and information, orchestrating relationships, and facilitating collaboration as a mentor or a coach.

- Increased expectations for availability, accountability, and productivity will eventually erode the barrier between work and personal life, forcing businesses to place greater emphasis on the balance between the two.

## Keeping an Eye on Governmental Direction

By the time governments begin to embrace and integrate new technologies into their operations, you can reasonably assume that those technologies have been in use long enough to be deemed firmly established. For example, since many transactions with governmental organizations are shifting toward electronic and IP-based systems, you could say that we are well into the e-world. Given that wireless technology is emerging in many local governments and military organizations, you could hypothesize that we are not far from entering the m-world. Businesses prepared for this eventuality will be best positioned to take advantage and even steer the development of these technologies for their own benefit. They will also be ready to adjust their policies if legislators should tighten the regulations on mobile or virtual working relationships to protect citizens.

## Components of a Mobilized Business

Mobilizing a business is not a matter of simply equipping the sales force with gee-whiz handheld devices. Evolving to a mobilized business requires a holistic approach. Ignoring any of the components shown in Figure 3 could seriously jeopardize the potential gains of transitioning to a mobilized business.

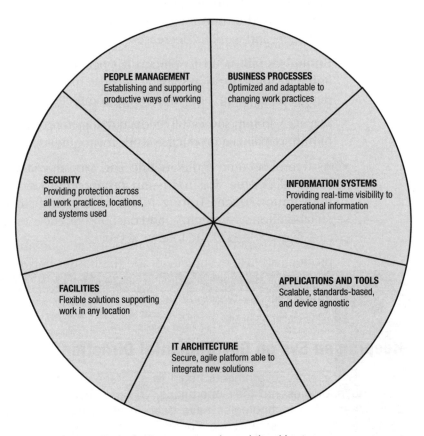

Figure 3. Components of a mobilized business.

A successful mobilized business will account for these components in the following ways:

- Business processes and systems allow the organization to access and interact with corporate information on an as-needed basis from selected mobile business devices.

- Scalable, standards-based applications and tools enable routine and specialized work tasks on mobile devices.

- The IT architecture provides secure access to information over a robust mobile device platform that fully integrates with existing solutions and mobile technologies.

- Well-defined security policies and their enforcement ensure that corporate information remains confidential and protected regardless of location.

- Flexible workplaces and workplace solutions facilitate and support mobile workers while in the corporate office, at home, in transit, or at a remote site.

- People management practices support and encourage 1) new ways of working and 2) the management and development of mobile workers and virtual teams.

These components all fall within the commonly accepted categories of people, business, and technology. Any mobility initiative must successfully address these three different perspectives. These perspectives and the consequences of ignoring them are summarized in the following table.

| | People | Business | Technology |
|---|---|---|---|
| **Major interests** | Simple, intuitive solutions<br>I choose when, where, and how I work | Growth, productivity, competitive advantage, improved customer service, return on investment, and usage metrics | Cost efficiency in implementation and use<br>Continuity among technologies to protect investments<br>Project is under control |
| **What they want** | Appropriate and easy access wherever I am | Cost-effective solutions that meet business and user needs | A scalable, secure, and interoperable infrastructure that meets business and user needs |
| **Consequences of ignoring perspective** | Lack of adoption, resistance, low usage levels<br>Benefits of mobility are not realized | Lost opportunities to reduce costs, increase worker productivity, and establish competitive advantage through a more responsive customer service system<br>Business case often not achieved | High implementation, integration, and operational costs<br>Information security risks |

As Nokia has begun evolving toward more mobile ways of working, focusing on each of these areas has helped us maintain a balanced approach between the people involved in our business, the processes that enable that business, and the technology that facilitates communication on the go. We have learned that focusing too much on any one area minimizes the benefits derived from the other areas. Keeping this holistic approach in mind has kept us from wandering too far from the path.

# The Executive's View of a Mobilized Business

From an executive's point of view, evolving to a mobilized business would result in an organization with the following characteristics:

- Mobile technologies are an integral part of the corporate IT infrastructure.

- Corporate information is appropriately secured across locations, systems, and work practices.

- New capabilities are achieved by adding mobile elements to business processes.

- Global and intercompany task forces can form quickly and work efficiently.

- The role of the corporate office and dependence on a nine to five time window diminish, providing the freedom to work where and when it is most convenient.

- Physical space is used for productive face-to-face work.

- Employees have more balance between work and personal life.

The following chapters expand this view of a mobilized business, providing the background, understanding, and tools needed to successfully assess an organization's mobility needs and to prepare solid mobility solutions.

## Things to Consider

- Mobility is the next step in the natural evolution of doing business. In some ways, mobility is already a part of doing business, and its role will only become stronger. Is your business ready to become more mobile? Why?

- How far is your business already mobilized? How far do you want to go?

- How will access to the right information at the right time regardless of location give you a competitive advantage?

- Mobility is more than gadgets and technology: it is a fundamental change in the way we work and manage work. As you begin to explore ways to incorporate mobile elements into your business, carefully consider the impact that mobility will have on workers, processes, and the IT infrastructure.

- How do you intend to balance your mobility strategy between people, processes, and technology?

- Think about your organization. What would business decision makers want from a mobility initiative? What would their concerns be? Apply the same questions to a typical end user and to your IT director.

# 3

# The Skeptics Speak: Challenges to Mobility

*People tend to over-mystify mobility because it is a new phenomenon fraught with challenges. However, once you spend the time to really understand what mobility is and what it can do for your business, there is really nothing mystical about it. When you combine the right technology with the right business processes and keep the user's perspective in mind, you greatly increase the likelihood of success for your mobility initiatives. If there is a magical element to mobility, it is decisiveness. You have to decide to go mobile and then stay committed as you face its challenges, or you will not see its benefits.*

*—Timo Kallioniemi, VP of Management Solutions*
*Nokia Business Infrastructure*

*This is a difficult challenge*—Finnish for *Are you crazy?* Even though Nokia is known as the mobility company, the idea of mobilizing Nokia itself was widely challenged by its own employees. Just mentioning the mobility initiative was likely to elicit comments like the following:

*"Those mobility guys are nuts. They haven't even considered how we're going to support a scattered workforce using devices that aren't standardized and that can't be remotely upgraded."*

*"I am highly skeptical of the claimed increases in productivity by moving to virtual teams. We are more likely to lose productivity as people cease working face to face."*

*"This new Communicator thing looks cool, but it's really just another ploy to eat up more of my free time. I can already hear my boss: 'I don't care if you're on the beach. You've got access to the information—just get me the answer I need now!'"*

*"I really don't see how mobility is going to reduce our costs— the connection fees for mobile devices alone will consume any potential savings in office space."*

*"If they are serious about mobility, they are going to have to look at processes and systems that touch almost every group in the company. What a nightmare!"*

The bottom line? Many people believed that business mobility at Nokia was "mission: impossible." There were simply too many barriers, hurdles, and unknowns.

When executives asked why the mobility initiative was not gaining traction, the response they received boiled down to this: "You want to understand why these projects aren't progressing? Listen to your managers. They're saying that it can't be done, and they're raising a lot of good points. We believe that mobilizing Nokia's business is the right thing to do, but we can't answer them when they ask how we intend to address these challenges." This response sparked an open, highly productive conversation about how to tackle the mobility challenges that emerged from Nokia's collective "voice of the skeptic."

How do you establish and maintain consensus in an environment where the people your project is intended to benefit don't believe you can succeed?

Ironically, gathering and presenting the challenges to mobility actually increased all-around interest in and support for the initiatives. Acknowledging the challenges generated support because it created a general feeling that Nokia's management was really listening to what people were saying. What had seemed to be insurmountable challenges became signs of progress along the mobility path.

# Understanding the Voice of the Skeptic

Why were so many of Nokia's employees skeptical of mobility? The underlying issue was change. Generally, people resist change because of the perception that it requires extra effort, that it is difficult, or that they will have to unlearn a familiar or comfortable way of doing things. This perception makes change the greatest challenge associated with mobility.

To realize the full value of mobilizing a business, it is important to recognize this challenge and address change management issues such as unwillingness to change work habits, disruption of developed communication methods, changes in where people work, and so on. For example, if sales people are going to adopt mobile work routines, the new processes should enhance their current way of working and the technology should make it easy for them to follow the processes.

Because of its scope, change affects people, processes, and technology (Figure 4). Consequently, we decided to organize the mobility challenges according to these three categories. We believe that Nokia's experience in identifying and describing these challenges can help other organizations as they begin to analyze their own mobility challenges.

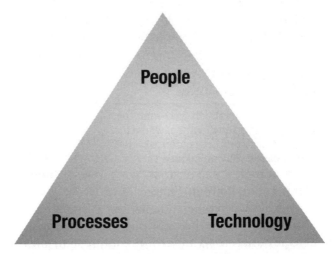

Figure 4. Change affects people, processes, and technology.

## People Challenges

People challenges affect the organization as well as mobile and traditional workers. The effects of these challenges can be far-reaching and often are not immediately obvious. We have categorized the main people challenges we have discovered as follows:

- Competency
- Management
- Workplace
- Operational support
- Self-management
- Family

### Competency Challenges

Effective mobile work requires certain competencies from individuals, managers, and teams. Unfortunately, not every employee has the competencies to operate effectively in a mobile environment. These competencies include communication skills and protocols, trust and trustworthiness, prioritization skills, and self-management skills.

Training and practice normally improve the situation, but even with training, some people are just not suited for mobile work habits. The challenge lies in finding ways to identify these competencies in employees and developing processes and programs to address and support employees who are at different points in adopting mobile work practices.

### Management Challenges

The people management challenges associated with mobility are quite complex. Given that, we mention them briefly here and elaborate on them in Chapter 9.

One of the greatest challenges is identifying mobile workers and dealing with the ramifications as organizations begin to classify roles as more or less mobile. Because most traditional management practices are not well suited for remote working situations, developing new habits that create a sense of trust between managers and workers, as well as creating systems and policies that support and encourage high performance in mobile roles, are very important activities.

Management skills like purpose and direction setting, coaching, managing to outcomes, networking, and managing change are paramount in a mobilized business, but it can be challenging to find managers that already possess these skills or to train existing managers in them.

Team dynamics also change as traditional teams adopt mobile work patterns. Managing expectations for acceptable work days, trying not to intrude on workers' personal lives, and maintaining informal and formal communication channels are just some of the challenges that arise from this transition.

### Workplace Challenges

Mobility changes the places where work gets done and business is conducted. Mobile workers spend more time working on the road and at home, reducing time spent at the office. The time that workers do spend at the corporate office is consumed in meetings rather than in individual work. In addition, mobile workers spend a larger percentage of time working at corporate premises other than those where they are based. These work patterns will change the way corporate real estate is used, with a shift toward collaborative areas and drop-in spaces (unassigned areas available for visitors).

Not addressing these changes early in mobility planning may cause significant problems in the future. For example, having more employees adopt mobile work modes while continuing to allocate corporate office space according to traditional methods (e.g., a cube for each local worker) will likely result in a chronic lack of available meeting rooms and visitor workspaces. Workers who remain in the office may begin to feel isolated when seats next to them are empty most of the time. Leasing or buying new office space to counterbalance the problem simply undermines the business case. Worse still, if changes to seating allocation are done half-heartedly, mobility projects can get labeled as nothing more than space-saving projects. Ideas for dealing with these and other workplace challenges are presented in Chapter 8.

### Operational Support Challenges

Supporting mobility initiatives may produce extra work for other functions, including IT, human resources, facilities, and security. If these departments see mobility as extra work for their scarce resources, with the benefits going to other departments, needed support for mobility initiatives may dry up quickly. Identifying compelling reasons for these people to take on the extra work (perceived or real) that mobility generates is vital to gaining their support. The same thing holds true for convincing a business unit to invest in mobility when the benefits of mobility may accrue to other units and departments. Chapter 10 suggests how to deal with this challenge when developing a business case.

### Self-Management Challenges

Working mobile requires a stronger level of self-discipline than traditional work. Mobile workers will face varying degrees of difficulty handling the self-management challenges outlined in the following table.

| Typical Comment | Associated Challenge |
| --- | --- |
| I'll just reply to this email now—it's only 2:00 am. | Knowing when to stop working |
| I'm at the pool with my kids on a Saturday…do I have to review this spreadsheet? | Controlling the guilty feeling of having to work 24/7 because mobile devices function almost anywhere |
| How do I develop a productive relationship with a disembodied voice? | Developing skills for working with people that you rarely meet face to face |
| I read email as soon as I get the notification about a new message—no matter what I'm doing. It lets me respond to requests quickly, but I don't feel very productive with my main work tasks. | Controlling push email's addictive effects |
| I know I should be able to work in any quiet place, but I have a hard time concentrating if I'm not in the office where I'm used to working. | Learning to work in different locations |
| I'll get to my work as soon as I move this batch of laundry around. | Avoiding the distractions of home |
| This is great! Now that I'm not in a cube at the office, no one can see that I haven't got a clue what I'm doing. I think I'll just go play some golf and work on my swing. | Hiding from your work |
| I always have my mobile with me; no one will mind if I give my email address and phone number to my soccer team. | Avoiding the temptation to use company resources for private needs |

Businesses will have to work carefully to plan for these challenges and help their employees overcome them. Typically this is best done by working closely with the human resources department.

### Family Challenges

Mobile work can blur the boundaries between family and work. However, blurred boundaries are nothing new, since the separation of work and family life is a relatively recent byproduct of the nineteenth century's industrial age. However, the real challenge is that members of a worker's family and household are confronted with their loved one being in a new role. Suddenly, kids are saying, "Daddy doesn't go to the office any more—he hides out in the basement and comes up to eat lunch with us. Now he can play with us more often." Or you may hear things like, "Wherever we go, Mom is always talking on her phone or sending email. It's like she isn't even with us."

Several members of the team that developed this book experienced these challenges first-hand. The wife of one of the authors once said to her husband, "Life used to be much more predictable. You went to work in the morning and came home in the evening. Now I do not always know when you are coming or going, or when you are in the middle of a phone conference at home. It is becoming more difficult for me to plan my life." Family challenges are most dangerous because they threaten to upset an important source of stability for most people.

## Process Challenges

When dealing with processes, the challenge lies in deciding which processes 1) are the best candidates for mobilization and 2) have the greatest likelihood of being adopted by the affected workers. Even though a process may appear to be an excellent candidate for mobility, it will probably not be successful if the workers do not follow the process. Chapter 6 discusses how to handle these and other business process challenges.

> When your business priority is cost reduction, mobility may be seen as an expensive case with minimal added value in the short term.

An associated challenge is developing a solid case that convinces stakeholders to mobilize one or more processes. As with any business case, those with more straightforward bottom-line benefits are more likely to be approved and funded.

Yet another challenge often crops up during implementation: if the implementation period is long and the business case is not realized quickly enough, the project risks losing consensus. This can result in accusations of not realizing the stated benefits, threats to cancel the implementation, or worst of all, having mobility projects labeled as difficult cases that are to be avoided.

## Technology Challenges

Technology challenges often overlap with the other two kinds of challenges, but their root cause or solution usually lies in technology. Compared to people challenges, technology challenges tend to change over time. For example, until recently, data speed has been a significant technology challenge, but new developments are rapidly solving that problem. However, those same developments can bring new challenges that will need to be resolved. Chapter 7 addresses many of the challenges described briefly below.

### Technology Selection Challenges

Mobile technology itself can be a challenge. In 2005, we have a range of mobility options: different wireless standards, different operating systems, and different screen resolutions in mobile devices. Understandably, this situation can create uncertainty and doubt among business decision makers. The challenge lies in determining whether the risk of delaying a decision until later outweighs the potential benefits of adding mobile capabilities now.

### Mobile Carrier Service Challenges

The larger the geographic footprint of a company, the more difficult it is to find a one-stop shop carrier. In fact, for a global company, working with a single carrier is currently impossible. Other challenges related to mobile carriers include billing systems that do not support all corporate needs, a general lack of acceptable service level agreements, and effective ways of measuring those service levels.

### IT Support Challenges

Also of concern are the IT support issues that arise as more mobile functions are added to an organization's infrastructure. For example, handling device diversity, providing 24/7 help desk support for mobile workers (who are often in non-traditional locations), and guaranteeing the quality of wireless coverage and service can all pose significant challenges.

### Application Design Challenges

A common technology challenge is figuring out how to get legacy and turn-key solutions to interface with newer mobile technologies. Integrating a legacy accounting application to deliver to or accept data from mobile devices can result in a variety of complications, including accounting for differences in screen size and resolution, adapting to touch screen input, and so on.

Integrating with mobile devices also has the potential to increase the complexity of troubleshooting because there are more layers of technology infrastructure to manage (device, device operating system, application, wireless network, etc.). Also, if the user interface of a mobile device or application is poorly designed, or if users feel that the interface does not serve its purpose, there may be user adoption challenges.

### Security Challenges

In a mobilized company, sensitive information is handled and stored outside of the secure corporate premises. Without proper policies, training, and enforcement, companies face the risk of security breaches. Mobile device and data encryption, which are essential for mobile security, also add to the list of security challenges.

# Letting Workers Identify Challenges

When Nokia internally piloted a solution for entering time card information into a mobile device and then synchronizing the information with a legacy time reporting system, most participants felt that the mobile capability added value. Recording hours in a mobile device made it easier for workers to take care of this administrative task. It also enhanced the way time card information was reported, leading to more accurate and timely reporting. However, some participants dropped out of the pilot because of challenges with the application's design. These workers made comments such as the following:

- "Everything went fine as long as I used the standard activities. But when I wanted to add an activity to the timesheet, the troubles started."

- "I have so many activities that the list is really long. Scrolling back and forth with the mobile interface takes too much time—it is much faster to do it on a large screen."

- "I always get the error message: 'Could not find specified internet server'."

While frustrating for the pilot participants, their comments helped the application designers identify and eventually resolve the design challenges.

### Cost Management

Managing the operational costs of mobile solutions can be very challenging. For example, the cost structures for mobile network access can vary widely and actual costs can be unpredictable because users are not always aware of the charges associated with using their mobile devices.

To illustrate, suppose that a Nokia employee from Finland on a business trip to France gets bored and, just out of curiosity, decides to download a four gigabyte, DVD-quality movie into his internet-enabled 3G phone over the mobile network. In summer 2005, and unbeknownst to him, the roaming data cost of that download would have been €11.00 per megabyte, resulting in an approximate charge of €44,000.00.

# A Coordinated Response

The larger the company, the more mobility can have far-ranging effects throughout the organization. Coordinating the response to mobility challenges is key to overcoming them. For an effective response, the people driving a mobility initiative must have access to all levels of the organization and have the authority to ensure that all efforts are synchronized. In Nokia's case, this meant giving the mobility team the authority to do the following:

- Identify the solutions, processes, programs, projects, and communities that would be affected by mobilization.

- Coordinate how each of these areas would go through the mobilization process.

- Ensure that each mobility initiative would be successfully completed.

In the end, it became the team's responsibility to identify and deal with all of the mobility challenges at Nokia.

## The Ripple Effect

Mobility initiatives are very similar to any other large-scale change where processes, people's behaviors, and supporting IT systems have to be modified. For example, Nokia sales representatives requested real-time, mobile access to customer revenue histories. Because they already had versatile mobile devices, getting real-time access to important information ought to have been as easy as reaching into the existing IT system and pushing the information to the device. From the sales representatives' point of view, this was an important way to increase sales, and it seemed like a simple request. That, however, was not the case.

Because the customer information was sensitive and could not be compromised, the connection between the mobile device and the information store had to be secure. This meant determining how to enable encryption support on the mobile device as well as finding the best way to secure the data pipe. The application that held the customer revenue histories had not been designed to allow this type of data access, so the database structure had to be changed to allow users to pull specific information about a specific customer. Once these changes were implemented, the solution would be in place, and everyone would be happy, right?

Wrong. After implementing mobile access to the appropriate data, it became apparent that the customer information was not up to date. It turned out that the sales representatives only sporadically captured and updated this information—usually to comply with monthly reporting requirements. To reap the benefits of real-time access to customer revenue histories, the sales representatives had to change their work practices and behaviors to support more active reporting to the database.

When sales representatives finally got this more accurate information, they felt they would benefit by having the same type of access to other customer-specific information. Expanding from a simple revenue history to more complete information about a customer (most recent orders and shipping dates, for instance) would require investigating other business processes like demand-supply balancing, the ways those processes were managed, their effect on current work behaviors, and so forth. The point here is that, like a stone dropped in a pool of water, even the smallest requirement in a mobility project can cause far-reaching ripples (Figure 5).

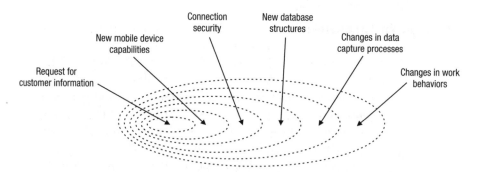

Figure 5. The ripple effect of a simple mobility request.

This exercise, conducted early in Nokia's mobility initiative, helped everyone involved understand that the challenges of mobility are varied, complex, and often not immediately obvious. Given that, some people may wonder, "If it's so complex, why even bother? Wouldn't it just be easier to forget about mobility and continue doing business as usual?"

Nokia's answer would be: "It depends on your business needs." To answer that question, business decision makers should be asking themselves these kinds of questions:

- Where does it make sense to mobilize my business?

- How do I want to position my business with respect to mobility? On the leading edge, in the mainstream as things stabilize, or near the end, avoiding the change for as long as possible?

- What steps can I take now to ease the transition to mobility when we are ready to make the move?

- What knowledge can we extract from existing mobility pilots and implementations?

Nokia recognizes that mobility creates short-term instability by uncovering a plethora of process, people, and technology challenges. But it also brings many benefits, some of which will only become apparent after mobility becomes the standard way of doing business.

## Things to Consider

Mobility is a holistic solution that requires cross-functional collaboration as you address people, process, and technology challenges.

- What actions can you take to include your workforce (and especially line managers who will be managing mobile workers) in the process of identifying and overcoming challenges to proposed mobility initiatives?

- What parts of your organization will need to be involved in planning, preparing for, and managing resistance to the changes that mobility will bring to established work patterns?

- Look for ways to turn mobility challenges into positive milestones that show progress.

- Consider using a ripple effect diagram to extrapolate and anticipate changes that mobilization will bring to your business.

# 4

# Identifying the Benefits of Mobility

*The world's moving faster, and so is information. Mobility cuts the tether of location, letting me work anytime and anywhere. It helps me keep ahead of my business.*

*—John Robinson, Senior VP of Services, Operations, and Quality*
*Nokia Enterprise Solutions*

We have some good news and some bad news. Which would you like to hear first? The good news? Okay. Identifying benefits and building a business case for point mobility solutions is pretty easy. The bad news? Identifying benefits and building a case for horizontal mobility solutions can be pretty tough. Why, you ask, is one so much harder than the other?

Point, or vertical, mobility solutions generally address a very specific need for a small, vertical segment of the organization. They address a frequently obvious pain point, are tied to a process or application specific to that part of the organization, and usually include compelling benefits in terms of cost reduction or revenue growth. For example, sending work orders directly to a cable repair technician's mobile device instead of having him return to the office to pick up new orders can reduce time and costs. Similarly, introducing the ability to use the mobile device to accept credit card payments while at a customer site can increase cash flow by reducing the billing cycle. Solutions such as these present obvious benefits and provide almost immediate return.

Horizontal mobility solutions, on the other hand, lay the foundation for a mobilized business. They usually require a significant investment that may not generate an immediate return. At Nokia, for instance, the mobility team encountered some resistance to a proposal to build a wireless local area network (WLAN) infrastructure on one of the corporate campuses. The initial investment was significant, and there were few immediate financial benefits. The project was only approved after the team explained that the WLAN would lay the foundation for other vertical solutions, such as scanning parts information directly from the loading dock into a back-end inventory system using a mobile device and the WLAN.

The bottom line is that, if an organization wants to transform itself into a mobile business, it has to identify benefits and build cases for both kinds of mobility solutions. The rest of this chapter discusses how the mobility team went about doing this at Nokia.

# Finding a Precedent

When the mobility team sat down to define the benefits of adding horizontal and vertical mobile capabilities to Nokia's business operations, they knew they could not articulate all the benefits in a spreadsheet. So what did they do? They looked to the past for a similar situation.

The first thing that came to mind was email. When it first became available, no one could build a rock-solid business case around email—they could not even decide how to spell it. Why? Because, at the beginning, no one could say with any degree of certainty how this new technology would actually be used.

Consider the evolution of email: although many people initially resisted this informal, written form of communication because it seemed more complicated than just picking up the phone, they soon realized that using email could mitigate risks by creating a paper trail of decisions. As familiarity with email increased and the technology improved, it evolved into a common business communication tool. Now, one trend is that people use their inbox rather than their computer's traditional folder system to store files because leaving the files with the accompanying email provides a context that the folder system does not offer. After a couple of decades of using email as a business tool, no one would dispute its benefits: streamlined communication, improved collaboration in a distributed workforce, use of the inbox as backup storage for files, and so on.

What did looking at the history of email give Nokia's mobility team? A basis for extrapolating how mobile capabilities could evolve (and, ironically, a good example of how mobility can improve an existing technology like email). The team chose to assume that mobility would follow a trajectory similar to email: from i nitial resistance to gradual acceptance to pervasive use as a standard business tool. This assumption allowed the team to begin to develop scenarios and identify potential benefits for mobility solutions based on the email experience.

# General Business Benefits

The mobility team did not delay in identifying general business benefits that would result from adding mobile elements to Nokia's operations. The team mapped these benefits according to whether they were financial or non-financial, quantifiable or non-quantifiable (Figure 6).

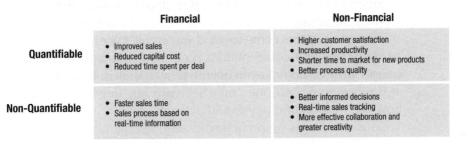

Figure 6. General business benefits of mobility.

The process of identifying these general benefits revealed ways that Nokia's major stakeholders would be positively affected by the mobility initiatives. For example, one quantifiable, non-financial benefit involved taking advantage of traditional downtime like commuting and traveling to produce a higher level of productivity among workers. Employees would also enjoy a better quality of life and would be more satisfied with their performance because mobile tools would provide greater flexibility in their work—an attractive, although non-financial, intangible benefit.

For executives, having right-time access to relevant, high-quality information would promote faster and better-informed decision making—a compelling assumption even though there was no obvious way to measure its financial impact. In addition, the amount of paper-based and manual work in business processes could be reduced, improving efficiency and accuracy in the processes—a quantifiable financial benefit. Although the extent of this benefit was unknown in the beginning, most people agreed that Nokia's improved ability to maintain contact and provide customer service would result in more satisfied customers and increased sales.

As the team drilled down into the potential impact of mobile capabilities on Nokia's business, they delineated more detailed benefits and value areas, some qualitative, others quantitative. This exercise allowed the team to begin developing ways to measure quantitative benefits, and scenarios that would illustrate qualitative benefits. The following table outlines how specific types of benefits result from adding mobile functionality to business activities.

Of course, it goes without saying that the identified benefits have to be realistic: you probably cannot claim that adding mobile capabilities to your field service force will end world hunger. But if you are the Red Cross, you could reduce lag time in updating situation reports during disasters by equipping workers with mobile devices that send information directly to back-end reporting and monitoring systems. The benefits of mobility are abundant: you just have to identify them and then clearly define whether they are quantifiable or non-quantifiable, financial or non-financial.

| Qualitative | | Quantitative | |
|---|---|---|---|
| **Identified Benefit** | **Results from...** | **Identified Benefit** | **Results from...** |
| More data accuracy | Better control of information | More efficient use of working time | Reduced travel time<br><br>Less time spent on paperwork<br><br>Less time spent on service<br><br>Faster work completion time<br><br>More visits per day |
| Better service | Faster access to information<br><br>Quicker responses to customer requests (e.g., order fulfillment) | Reduced need for support resources (e.g., data entry) | Data sent directly to back-office systems |
| Better planning and decision making | Right-time, fact-based information | Faster time to market | Faster deliveries<br><br>Increased new and renewal sales |
| Better working experience | Increased relevance and value of individual's knowledge<br><br>Better spirit and morale<br><br>Enhanced collaboration<br><br>Enhanced learning | Improved cash flow | Reduced billing cycles |

# Pitching the Benefits of Mobility

Having identified a good set of general business benefits, the team began looking for a way to organize the mobility benefits in a measurable, standard format. Because proposed mobility solutions had to follow Nokia's standard project approval process, the team decided to frame the benefits they identified by using a scorecard system with the following categories:

- Financial
- People
- Process
- Customer

The rest of this chapter presents a summary of the main benefits that the mobility team identified. Some benefits occur in multiple categories: this simply emphasizes the fact that benefits—be they for mobility or other projects—generally affect several dimensions of an organization.

## Financial Benefits

Financial benefits are what everyone wants to see—the more tangible, financial benefits in a business case, the more likely decision makers are to approve the project. In Nokia's experience, mobility can positively affect the bottom line through revenue growth and cost reduction.

### Revenue Growth

Improvements in employee performance, sales, and product delivery ultimately lead to revenue growth. For example, giving sales people mobile, right-time access to customer information allows them to act more quickly on potential opportunities. Adding mobile capabilities to logistics functions can result in faster time to market, faster deliveries to customers, and higher customer satisfaction. These positive outcomes produce more new and renewal sales, and directly improve revenue growth.

One important area where mobile capabilities make significant contributions to the bottom line is in improving cash flow. Typically in non-mobile business processes, a customer orders a product or service, waits a long time to get the bill, and then pays. This process contributes to billing cycles of 30 to 60 days or longer. Adding mobile capabilities to internal billing processes can dramatically reduce billing times, resulting in improved cash flow—a very tangible business benefit. For instance, equipping customer service technicians with mobile devices that can capture customer payment information and send it directly to back-office billing systems would significantly reduce the time spent using a traditional paper-based billing process.

While measuring the exact financial impact of mobility (for example, determining how much sales growth can be attributed to a mobility project) is more difficult than calculating reductions in costs, measuring improvement can provide a good estimate.

### Cost Reduction

Giving workers the ability to access information and communicate wherever they are can result in significant cost savings as well. For example, equipping virtual teams with the tools they need to stay in touch and be productive can reduce the need for frequent travel. In spite of a tenfold increase in international interaction, Nokia has been able to contain internal travel costs in the new millennium by providing access to virtual and mobile conferencing systems.

We have also been able to reduce telecommunications costs at many sites by moving to the mobile phone as the only phone. Obviously, maintaining a fixed phone and a mobile phone is more expensive—not only because of double carrier costs but because calls between fixed and mobile phones are more expensive than mobile-to-mobile calls. A relatively new mobile capability called Fixed-to-Mobile Convergence (FMC) lets mobile phones roam between the corporate telecom network and external carriers, depending on where the worker is located. By negotiating favorable rates with external carriers, businesses may be able to realize a significant reduction in their overall telecom budget.

In Sweden, Nokia moved to a mobile voice infrastructure that increased the company's mobile phone bill. But controllers were not worried, because total annual voice costs dropped by 38%.

Mobility can also lead to real estate savings for companies because, as workers become more mobile, office use changes. It is possible to harness that change and reduce the overall amount of space needed for individual work, thus reducing the need for as many fixed assets. Nokia has found that double-digit savings on overall real estate costs are achievable, but not without addressing the interlinked people challenges. (This topic is discussed more thoroughly in Chapter 8.)

## Taking a Good Look at Benefits

Talk to any Voice over Internet Protocol (VoIP) phone manufacturer and cost savings will come up. However, in an internal study carried out at Nokia on VoIP desk phones, we found that the cost savings from desk phone calls were greatly diminished because mobile workers were forwarding calls made to their desk phones to their mobile phones. Because the forwarding service was relatively expensive, we could not realize the expected savings. Nokia concluded that, although VoIP can be useful in some circumstances (with international routing, for example), VoIP presents the greatest benefits when it is wireless.

## People Benefits

The benefits of mobility on the people aspects of an organization are numerous and far-reaching. Most of these benefits tend to be non-financial and qualitative. However, as many organizations have come to realize, investments in human capital, while not always easy to capture in a spreadsheet, are often the difference between success and failure. As Nokia has experimented with adding more mobile capabilities to our workforce, we have found benefits that express themselves through increased employee satisfaction and motivation.

### Increased Employee Satisfaction

Increased employee satisfaction grows from improved work environments and a healthy balance between work and personal life. Because mobility puts information, tools, and people at workers' fingertips regardless of their location or the time of day, employees they are suddenly presented with a multitude of options for how to get their work done. For example, when a sales person who travels frequently gets home, the last thing she wants to do is sit down and transcribe her customer visit notes. Giving her a mobile device that lets her enter notes during or immediately after each visit and then send the information directly to the company's customer relationship management (CRM) system will cause her satisfaction level to skyrocket.

This freedom to get work done on one's own terms—of no longer being tied to a specific place or time—creates undeniable benefits that, until recently, were simply not an option for many workers. Consider people who have long commutes on public transportation. Mobility turns wasted commute time into productive working time: using their mobile devices, employees can approve expense reports and time cards, catch up on email, and download materials for morning meetings. Car commuters can combine work at home with corporate office work to avoid peak traffic hours and still be productive—or they can switch to a home office to avoid the commute altogether.

About 60 km south of Nokia's Haukipudas offices near Oulu, Finland, lies the town of Lumijoki, where a few of Nokia's employees live. They go to a satellite office in Lumijoki where they telecommute to the main office. This setup creates a win-win situation for everyone. Lumijoki retains its taxpayers. Employees do not have to waste time traveling and they can spend more time with their families. Having the option to work at a satellite office with access to all the tools they need to be productive instead of going to the corporate office generates an incredible amount of satisfaction in these employees.

Why does mobility create higher employee satisfaction? Because it enhances employees' ability to maintain a healthy balance between work and personal life. Family emergencies do not always happen outside of office hours, and work emergencies do not always take place between nine and five. The flexibility of choosing where and when to work creates harmony in what has become an increasingly cacophonous existence.

### Increased Employee Motivation

The corporate office can be a boring place. Not everyone can produce brilliant new ideas while stuck in a beige box with artificial lighting. Some people get their best ideas at strange hours. Other people find it very hard to concentrate in open office areas. The option of working somewhere outside the corporate cube farm and at some time other than traditional office hours increases the motivation to work. With a mobile device as simple as a laptop equipped with wireless network access, workers can seek out places that inspire their creativity, expand their thoughts, and provide a more focused work environment.

Offering workers mobile work options can also increase their commitment to the company. If workers sense that their managers trust them to get their job done without direct supervision, they are more likely to get that job done—usually better and in less time overall. This in turn boosts morale because personal productivity increases as workers accomplish more in the same amount of time. Nokia has found that employees who want and get more flexibility in their work routines tend to stay committed to the company. Leveraging mobile work as a tool for attracting and retaining talented employees can also reduce overall induction and training costs, which often run very high.

> Ironically, when work goes mobile, people may become less mobile because they can get their work done without moving from place to place.

As access to information at the moment of need becomes a standard paradigm for doing business, workers will independently seek out effective methods to stay on top of situations and to respond as needed. For example, with the help of Nokia One, an older internal service that transfers email into short message service (SMS) messages and vice versa, Nokia employees can receive an SMS notification on their mobile phones when email containing a pre-defined keyword arrives. The employees can go about their business, be it in their offices, around the corporate campus, or off-site, without having to check their email every five minutes. When they receive the SMS notification, they can immediately send a response via SMS or find somewhere to access their inbox and reply to the email.

Finally, mobility motivates groups of people that share common goals to stay connected and productive. Team flexibility increases when members and processes are mobile because communication is faster and teams work smarter. A case in point: a global mobile team worked on this book. In the final stages of writing the manuscript, one of the authors, who was living in Singapore, wrote content during his day. At the end of his day, he sent the content to Utah, in the western United States, where other team members were just beginning their day. They spent their day working on the author's content, sending it back in time for him to begin working the next morning, Singapore time. The team worked smarter by taking advantage of the 12-hour time difference to keep the creative process flowing almost non-stop.

## Process Benefits

The process category boasts the widest variety of benefits—tangible and intangible, quantifiable and non-quantifiable, financial and non-financial. The single greatest benefit of mobility to business processes where people, materials, and information are moving is the ability to improve performance by reducing slack, or non-productive time, in the process. Mobile capabilities do this by facilitating the flow of information in the process.

Consider how mobility can reduce slack in a service organization's billable time approval process. Employees submit their time in an online system, which sends a task to their manager to review and approve or reject the submission. If their manager is frequently away from the location where she has to do the approvals, the process can stay in limbo for days. The ability to access the online time system from a mobile device allows the manager to respond more quickly, potentially cutting days from the overall process, allowing the organization to tabulate billable hours and invoice its clients more quickly.

The improvements gained by adding mobile capabilities to business processes often translate into bottom-line business benefits of reduced costs, increased sales, and increased efficiency. We have grouped these benefits into two categories: 1) information capture and retrieval and 2) process efficiency.

## Save Time: Call People, Not Places

When you make a phone call to an individual's desk, you are calling a place, not a person. Since many workers spend less than 40% of their time at their desks, your chances of reaching people at their desks are not that good. If, in your business process, you call ten people's desk phones per day on average, statistics show that you will reach only four of the ten on the first attempt. On the second attempt, you will reach another three. On the third, two more. It will take you a fourth attempt to reach the last person. These repeated attempts add up to ten unnecessary phone calls, or ten wasted minutes out of 400 working minutes. If you request a call back to your desk phone, it is likely that you will not be there when the person returns your call.

If your business process requires only internal calls, equipping employees with just a mobile phone will reduce the time you spend trying to contact them because you will be calling a person, not a place. Of course, they still might not answer if, for example, they are in a meeting, but chances are greater that you will make contact with them on the first attempt. Two additional benefits of this change are that 1) having only one phone number is simpler and 2) using only a mobile phone can reduce overall telecommunication expenses when coupled with FMC technology.

### Information Capture and Retrieval

Recording information directly into a mobile device rather than on paper produces several benefits. First, accuracy increases because information is not entered into the system multiple times. Second, because the person entering the information understands its relevance, the quality of the data improves. Third, entering information directly into a mobile device that interfaces with a back-end system can reduce the need for data entry resources. Finally, when data is transferred to back-end systems in near real-time, the time needed to provide information to those making business decisions is reduced, thus resulting in better-informed decision makers.

Mobile data capture and reporting have allowed Nokia to re-engineer its sales channel processes in China. Sales representatives and promoters working in the field capture information about Nokia and competitor product sales. They send this information—by using a Nokia mobile device, a tailored mobile application, and Global System for Mobile communications (GSM) data access—to an application server where it is made available for review and analysis. This internal information source gives Nokia sales management visibility into market trends, peak season phenomena, and changes in demand, enabling faster reactions and better management of people, business, and channel relationships.

In a similar way, being able to receive current business information on a mobile device leads to more informed decisions and increased customer satisfaction. For example, supplying technicians with the repair history and availability of spare parts for a product under service can result in more accurate decisions about how to repair the product, because the technicians have the most up-to-date information possible.

Two related mobile capabilities, telemetry and remote device management, allow companies to exchange information with devices in remote locations. In Sweden, for example, a mobile carrier and an electricity meter manufacturer offer an electricity meter that has an embedded GSM module and a subscriber identity module (SIM) card. Regardless of its location, the electricity meter can be read automatically over the mobile network. This type of mobile solution produces business benefits that include more productive workers, lower travel costs, and automated data entry.

## Fast Emergency Response

Receiving timely information about earthquakes on a mobile device gives Nokia's security organization the ability to react to potentially life-threatening situations on a moment's notice. Instead of waiting for popular media sources to announce an earthquake, Nokia monitors announcements from the United States Geological Survey Earthquake Hazards Program. When this service releases verified information about an earthquake—often only a few minutes after it happens—key security personnel receive a text message about the situation on their mobile devices. This near real-time process allows Nokia's security staff to immediately begin warning employees (as in the event of a tsunami warning) and coordinating required rescue efforts (as soon after the disaster as possible).

### Process Efficiency

Mobility improves process efficiency by reducing work steps and streamlining activities. In other words, it removes slack from processes. As mentioned throughout this book, when people are involved in processes, mobile technologies help deliver information from a process to people regardless of where they are. Being able to take care of routine activities such as reviews, approvals, and email leads to improved workflow and reduced idle time in business processes.

Nokia conducted an internal study on push email in the summer of 2005 and found that pilot users saved an average of 75 minutes per week by reading and responding to their email on a mobile device. The benefits were not limited to personal productivity. This is what one manager said about mobile email: "I have a global role. Push email lets me react quicker while people are awake in different time zones. This saves valuable days that would be lost by people not replying until they wake up the following day."

When materials are moving in a process, the quantifiable benefits of mobility come from replacing warehouses with information. Moving information instead of moving and stocking materials can lead to substantial savings. Benefits received from adding mobile capabilities to a process can include the following:

- Reduced inventories (a one-time positive cash flow effect)

- Reduced inventory carrying costs

- Fewer obsolete materials

- Faster order fulfillment

In addition, when a mobile fleet is part of a company's core, the ability to track the fleet, optimize routes, and assign tasks while the fleet is in motion offers quantifiable business benefits.

Providing information about the location of materials is another way that mobility can improve process efficiency. Using technologies such as Radio Frequency Identification (RFID) tags and global positioning system (GPS) information to communicate the accurate location of a specific item can create benefits in areas such as asset management, maintenance, repair, manufacturing, item tracking, delivery scheduling, customer billing, data collection, and work order management.

For instance, companies that offer waste disposal services could attach RFID tags to their waste containers to track each container's location, facilitate information gathering during inspections, and keep a record of inspections as proof of compliance with industry or governmental regulation. Each time an engineer inspects a container, he would scan the RFID tag and then record all relevant information from the inspection using a mobile device. Additionally, engineers could use the collected information to quickly identify which containers have failed inspection and then make plans about how to bring them into compliance.

### Customer Benefits

The financial, people, and process benefits described so far all generate a positive impact on customers. At Nokia, new mobile work habits and processes have reduced internal operating costs, in some cases leading to lower prices on the company's products and services.

We have seen how mobility improves communication: employees who work directly with customers become more accessible to them, while product development staff become more accessible to customer-facing employees. This enhanced communication has also improved response times for customer inquiries and requests. For example, we have been able to quickly form global ad-hoc teams to address customer problems—often outside of normal business hours—and then send solutions to the customer much more quickly than expected.

Adding mobile elements to Nokia's business processes has also helped our customer-facing employees be better informed about each customer's situation. For instance, because our sales representatives have right-time access to crucial customer information, they have been able to make last-minute changes to sales bids, thereby retaining existing relationships or starting new ones.

All of these benefits have led to increased customer satisfaction and stronger, longer-term relationships. Overall, we feel confident in saying that mobility has contributed to the positive results that Nokia is receiving on customer satisfaction surveys.

# Summary

Mobility offers quantitative and qualitative benefits, some immediately apparent, others yet to be discovered. In our experience, Nokia has seen and continues to see many benefits from its decision to add mobile capabilities to its business. These benefits fall into the categories discussed in this chapter—financial, people, process, and customer—and they produce many positive results, including reduced costs, increased revenues, improved customer satisfaction, and others. Taken together, these benefits of mobility have generated profitable growth for Nokia (Figure 7).

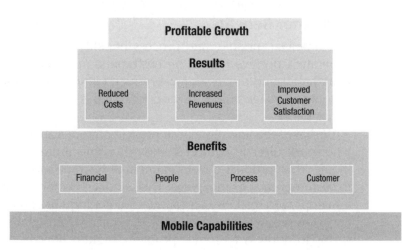

Figure 7. Mobile capabilities result in profitable growth.

We believe that the benefits of mobility will transform over time. The ones we have discussed in this chapter will probably not be the benefits that our workers enjoy in the future. But whatever the benefits may be, we are convinced that they will be tangible and compelling. And, as in the case of email, mobile ways of working will simply become a normal part of doing business.

## Things to Consider

Not all benefits can be quantified on financial statements—many benefits are intangible but still legitimate.

- How can adding mobile functions to your business improve employee and customer satisfaction and loyalty?
- Which areas of your IT organization could benefit from mobility? Could mobility decrease technology-related costs?
- Consider your organization's business processes. Which processes would make good candidates for adding mobile capabilities? What measurable benefits could you derive from mobilizing those processes?

# II

## Preparing for a Mobile Business

# 5

# Getting to Know Your Workforce

*If you don't account for user perspectives in your mobility strategy, you risk losing the support of the workforce—if you ever had it.*

*—Overheard at a Nokia mobility team meeting*

*Did we forget someone? Did we identify everyone who is going to be affected by mobility? Have we considered all perspectives?* These are questions that members of Nokia's mobility team asked themselves every day for months.

Past experience with user adoption efforts in other large-scale projects had convinced the team that to ensure the overall success of mobility at Nokia, they would have to include the workforce in the journey. They initiated activities to investigate and document workers' daily routines, work styles, typical work environments, information access needs, productivity barriers, and device constraints. By interviewing typical workers—asking questions and listening carefully to the answers—the team exposed many potential impacts that mobility would have on Nokia's business. As a result of these investigations, they concluded that much of the basic information used in Nokia's mobility initiatives would come directly from the workforce.

In this chapter, we present a digested version of the mobility team's efforts to understand Nokia's workforce. Even as we do this, the team continues to develop their techniques for understanding the people most affected by mobility. Why? To be more successful in their efforts to mobilize Nokia's business.

# Understanding Levels of Mobility

The mobility team's research led them to divide Nokia's workforce into four work types

- Light technology mobile

- Heavy technology mobile

- Campus mobile

- Non-mobile

These categories are driven primarily by the amount of time spent in travel and meetings. The following table profiles a typical worker from each work type.

| Work type | Time spent in travel | Time spent in meetings | Device-carrying preference | Preferred location | Typical role |
|---|---|---|---|---|---|
| Light technology mobile | Above 50% | Above 75% Primarily involved in decision making activities | Very little equipment Easy setup and takedown | Home when not traveling (to balance time spent away from family) | Executive Sales representative |
| Heavy technology mobile | Under 50% | About 50% Concentrated work sessions | Carry all necessary equipment | Home (to balance time spent away from family) | Field service worker Consultant |
| Campus mobile | Occasional travel outside office Move frequently between meeting rooms and campus locations | Above 50% Emphasis on information sharing | Carry all necessary equipment to present and capture information | Corporate campus Home as needed | Project manager Supply chain manager R&D worker |
| Non-mobile | Negligible Very little movement | Under 25% | Desk-based equipment | Dedicated office space | Assembly worker System designer |

The team also learned that Nokia's employees fell into one of eight predominant work styles. These work styles were defined based on the amount of travel, level of mobility when at a corporate site, type of interaction with colleagues, and primary mode of communication (Figure 8). These two ways of looking at Nokia's workforce—work types and work styles—gave the team a tool for quickly evaluating a worker's level of mobility. This, in turn, allowed the team to determine whether the person would be a good candidate for working in a mobile way.

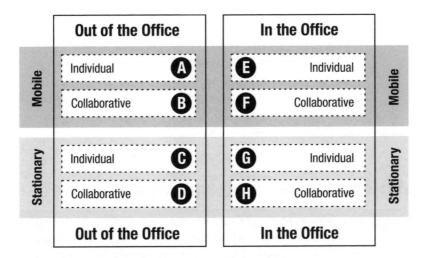

Figure 8. Typical work styles at Nokia.

One of the interesting outcomes of the workforce analysis was that workers with a certain work type tended to have similar work styles. What the team found were the following loose correlations:

- Employees with work styles A, B, C, and D tend to follow a *mobile* work type (either *light technology* or *heavy technology*).

- Employees with work styles E and F often have a *campus mobile* work type.

- Employees with work styles G and H are associated with *non-mobile* work types.

These tools have helped Nokia understand how its employees actually work. It has also helped Nokia predict the percentage of workers that would be affected by its mobilization efforts.

## Making Smart Mobility Decisions

One important result of the team's work was that, by knowing a worker's current level of mobility, they could ask the question, "How mobile should (or could) this person be?" For example, the team is currently discovering that employees who did not initially appear to benefit from mobile work practices are suddenly able to embrace mobility in unexpected ways. Therefore, it is good to be open-minded about new mobility opportunities. The team has also found that in some cases the management culture inhibits mobility even though work processes could easily be mobilized.

Expecting all workers to use mobile technologies might not always make sense. For example, some work styles include a large percentage of workers who could benefit from mobilized business processes, while others have relatively low percentages of workers who would immediately benefit from mobility. The key is to understand which workers can benefit the most from mobility and then begin building mobile functions and management practices into their daily work routines.

# Which Workers Are the Most Mobile?

In addition to identifying work types and work styles, the mobility team identified workers—or more specifically, communities of users—that seemed most likely to benefit from increased mobility in their work routines. The team arranged interviews with members of each community, with the following objectives:

- Understand each user community and its interfaces with other user communities

- Understand each community's daily work activities and chief pain points

- Identify mobility needs for each community and understand how those needs differ between communities

- Understand the impact of mobility on each community

- Gather data to help prioritize needs for each user community

The results of those interviews indicated that the user communities most likely to benefit from increased mobility in their work routines included the following:

- Leadership

- Sales and customer support (i.e., field forces)

- Program and project management

The roles in each community are mapped onto the main work types in Figure 9. In the figure, work types *light technology mobile* and *heavy technology mobile* are combined into the work type *mobile*. Within each community, different roles have differing mobility needs. For example, in the program and project management community, line managers typically work in a *mobile* mode more often than supply chain managers, who generally work in a *campus mobile* mode. Note, however, that even within one role, the type of work that the person performs can vary depending on, for instance, the geographical distribution of the team and the scale of responsibilities (as with project managers, who can be *mobile*, *campus mobile*, or *non-mobile*).

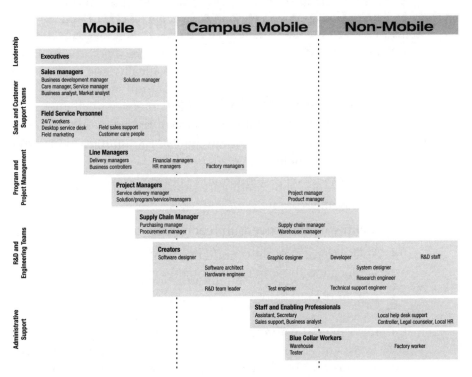

Figure 9. Mobile user communities.

## Listening to the Silent Majority

Nokia's mobility team faced a common situation: how do you successfully deliver on a top-down mandate when the value is unclear to middle management and bottom-up interest is unknown? The team had authority—they could use executive pressure to force cooperation. However, they knew that such an approach would guarantee the project's eventual failure. What they needed was a way to flip a top-down directive into a bottom-up initiative.

As they considered mobility at Nokia, one question kept coming up: "Who is affected by mobility and to what extent?" The team decided to interview workers across the company to build a deeper understanding of their needs and issues.

Although it was not their original intention, the mobility team became a user advocate group to upper management. By focusing on discovering how people worked, what their pain points were, and how mobility would affect the way they worked, the team embraced users and their perspective. In so doing, they gave employees a chance to express their concerns and comment on how they thought mobility would affect the company. Ordinary workers felt that their opinions would be taken into consideration and addressed appropriately in the corporate strategy. Because of their focus on the user, the team gave Nokia's employees a voice in the mobility process.

### Common Mobile Worker Needs

While each user community had its own unique work tasks, the team discovered that all communities had six common needs with respect to potential mobile work habits:

1. Access to email, calendar, and contacts

2. Access to corporate data and tools

3. Ability to collaborate with team members

4. Ability to receive alerts and critical information

5. Ability to show or present information quickly

6. Greater efficiency in reporting and approval processes

In retrospect, it was not surprising that these needs and related tasks were common to all mobile user communities. What was exciting was that by developing a relatively small set of mobile functions (e.g., one to two per activity), the team could fulfill the needs of the majority of mobile workers. The team chose to develop business cases for solutions that met these common needs first, leaving the remaining specialized work tasks and processes for further study and integration at a later date. As it turned out, many of those first cases were approved and have met with positive results.

# Understanding Mobile Worker Expectations

After the team had identified which groups of workers would be most likely to benefit from added mobility in their work patterns, they needed to understand worker expectations regarding the change to working mobile. After further study, the team identified the following top worker expectations and desires related to the shift toward a mobile work mode:

- Clear management expectations and measurements for individual performance while mobile

- Flexible work schedules to suit individual work patterns and life situations

- Quick access to team members and support for collaboration across sites and time zones

- Secure connectivity to business information regardless of location using standardized, IT-supported devices

- A local office or other approved location with all the tools, support, and resources needed to get special work done— without having to reconfigure devices

- Meeting rooms that can be quickly and remotely reserved when collaboration requires a planned or spontaneous face-to-face setting

Above all, it became clear that the responsibility for successfully mobilizing a business is shared between the business owner *and* the worker. In many cases, the impetus for more mobile work comes from the worker rather than the business. Nokia's experience has been that, at least in the beginning, more mobile work activities have been initiated by employees than by the business.

Regardless of who starts the discussion about becoming more mobile, both parties have to be flexible. At a minimum, employees should accept the need for change. Better still is if they feel a desire to work in a more mobile mode and then begin to actively adopt new ways of performing their work tasks. Businesses should also be flexible as they plan and implement mobility initiatives by learning about the workforce, understanding workers' current levels of mobility, appropriately accounting for cultural and individual differences, and adapting management practices.

> Focusing on solving real user problems with mobile technology creates a natural inclination in users to change the way they work.

At Nokia, we are discovering that understanding our workforce, their needs, and their expectations in terms of mobility gives us a clear direction for identifying business process candidates, making prudent technology choices, planning facilities infrastructure, and defining supportive management policies. This has been the very positive result of our decision to focus first on people's needs.

## Things to Consider

Understanding your mobile workers—their work types, work styles, and level of travel or movement—provides the best foundation for developing a successful business mobility strategy.

- How many workers are already mobile in your business?
- What business activities are common to most of your mobile workers?
- Are your workers ready to become mobile and to adopt new ways of working? Why?

Identifying different user communities among your workforce—and their biggest points of pain—will help you identify common needs and the best opportunities for mobilization.

- Which user communities could benefit from mobile ways of working?
- Which of your workers would achieve the greatest level of productivity through mobility? What are their biggest needs? How could mobility fulfill those needs?

Clarifying and accommodating mobile worker expectations will lead to wider change acceptance and quicker adoption of mobility in your business processes.

# 6

# Mobilizing Business Processes

*Like any other fast-moving company, we spend a lot of time and energy improving our business processes. A few years ago, we started to look at the effect of mobility on our processes. Our studies, trials, and implementations have taught us something important: mobility enables real-time information flow—the very core of an efficient business process. The really exciting part is that, with the mobile technologies available today, it really is possible to affordably streamline processes and significantly boost performance levels. As we holistically approach mobilizing business processes, we get a bit better every day: faster, leaner, more responsive, and more competitive.*

*—Aki Laiho, Head of Mobility Office*
*Nokia Business Infrastructure*

A lukewarm response. That is what the mobility team got when they presented their proposal for introducing mobile elements into the work practices of Nokia's field services personnel, sales representatives, and executives. This reaction threw the team off balance. What had gone wrong? Why could these people not see the obvious advantages of mobility in their work routines?

The team decided to step back and examine the situation. They had based their proposal on two major elements: 1) empirical evidence obtained from mobility deployments carried out in other companies, and 2) analysis of Nokia's workforce to gain insight into possible user communities and their associated business processes (see Chapter 5).

The team had also used productivity impact and risk of mobilization as screening criteria to generate a preliminary list of candidate processes. The results had seemed clear: focus on the parts of the organization that had natural needs for operating beyond the physical constraints of an office or desk environment. So why did the stakeholders from these groups not jump for joy when they saw the team's proposal?

What the team came to realize was that they had not been able to articulate compelling reasons why mobility was relevant to these groups. They had not been able to frame the mobility discussion within the context of the activities that these people performed every day. These shortcomings, combined with having to compete with other non-mobility initiatives for limited investment funds, prevented the team from making a strong case for mobility to Nokia's business owners.

# Identifying Business Processes for Mobilization

Determined to learn from their experience, the team turned to the underlying business processes to get at the heart of these people's activities. They began asking questions like the following:

- How do we identify processes where mobility can make a significant, positive difference?

- How can we translate this difference into easily understood business imperatives and thereby set the basis for robust business cases?

- Once we have identified a list of potential opportunities, how do we prioritize the target areas?

- How do we get started in a low-risk manner?

By concentrating on the business processes involved, by analyzing them in detail, and by developing profiles for them, the team was able to identify areas where mobility could provide clear, significant benefits. They also became increasingly aware that, to help Nokia's employees grasp the true power of mobility and become its champions within their business units, understanding Nokia's business processes was as crucial as understanding the people and the technology (Figure 10).

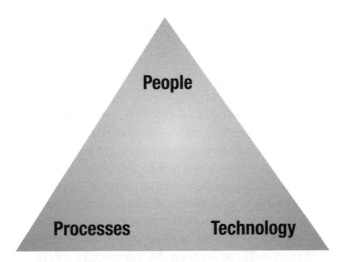

Figure 10. Crucial factors for successful mobility initiatives.

## Types of Business Processes

To understand Nokia's business processes in detail, the team interviewed 140 employees—including key process owners as well as stakeholders. These interviews opened a window into how the processes worked and provided a clearer level of insight into potential areas of opportunity.

As they analyzed the information gathered from the interviews, the team identified two general types of business processes that were in use at Nokia:

- Horizontal: These processes typically included the capabilities available to most Nokia employees—email, personal information management, voice, and telephony. In some cases, this list could be extended to include workflow and knowledge management tools. The key characteristic of these processes was that they were often vital to the point of being part of the business infrastructure. Without these enablers, the efficiency and efficacy of information exchange between employees, business units, and business processes would be woefully inadequate at best, and impossible at worst.

- Vertical: These processes encapsulated a distinct portion of Nokia's internal value chain—product development, manufacturing, supply chain, sales, customer service, and marketing. Due to the complex nature of these entities, it was fairly normal to break each of these processes down to manageable levels of complexity. For example, customer service could be further divided into support, warranty, field service, and so on.

In most cases, but especially with vertical processes, mobilization involved access to information that crossed traditional functional boundaries. For instance, mobilizing a field service process such as a telecommunications technician using a mobile device to manage daily activities would require access to customer data (address, service plan, and so on) as well as access to billing and invoicing information to ensure the completeness and quality of the service provided. This kind of cross-functional integration would also be needed when extending the field service capability to material and inventory tracking. A good example is a package delivery driver using a handheld device to track delivery confirmation and to provide frequent updates to the company's tracking application. This integration could extend to logistics and production planning as well.

## How Mobility Affects Business Processes

In a typical business process, a majority of the time involved in the process is spent in non-value-adding activities like waiting or traveling. Reducing this non-productive time, or slack, is key to improving business processes. Because information needed to move the process along is often inaccessible while the people or goods tied to that information are in motion, adding mobile capabilities can reduce slack and create a more rapid information flow (Figure 11).

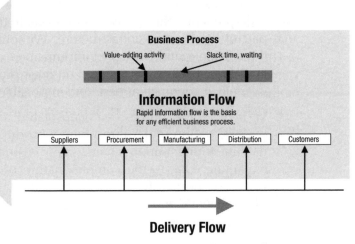

Figure 11. Business processes run on information flow.

The team wanted to target business processes where mobility offered the most attractive opportunities for reducing slack—whether through capturing information when it is created in the field or by asynchronously notifying personnel of relevant information to enable faster decision making. They were confident that by adding mobile capabilities to a business process they could achieve performance improvements and competitive advantages such as the following:

- Productivity improvements (i.e., reduction in costs and tied assets)

- Improved agility and responsiveness

- Improved customer service and new service opportunities

Mobility could improve the speed of information flow within Nokia's business and begin to move the company toward what has been called a "zero-latency" real-time enterprise.

## Profiling Business Processes

Given the large number of business processes that could potentially be mobilized—many of which spanned a full range of activities including demand creation, demand/supply chain, demand fulfillment, customer service, and project management—the team needed a method to profile processes for their suitability for mobilization. Such a method would yield an initial ranking of candidate processes that could then be explored with a detailed analysis and a business case.

The profiling method we present here is a slightly modified version of the one that the mobility team originally developed. The method's key characteristic is that it is simple and can be applied to practically any business process. It consists of assessing a business process across five dimensions:

- Workforce mobility

- Stakeholder interaction

- Information requirement

- Time to data

- Process maturity

Graphically mapping where a business process falls on each dimension creates a visual profile indicating the process's suitability for mobilization (Figure 12). Generally speaking, the higher a process falls on each dimension, the more likely it is to be a good candidate for some level of mobilization. Of course, the final decision on whether to mobilize a process should ultimately be made after considering all of the factors that influence the process.

Figure 12. The dimensions of a business process mobility profile.

In the rest of this section, we describe the dimensions and provide a series of questions for determining how to place business processes within them.

## Workforce Mobility

This dimension captures the percentage of the workforce that is mobile. It indicates the degree to which the workforce performs the business process outside the traditional physical boundaries of a business-computing environment. It also reflects the degree to which the workforce is expected to operate in an untethered environment due to the requirements of the business process. In this context, workers who spend more than 40% of their time away from their office environment would be considered mobile workers.

## Stakeholder Interaction

This dimension shows the degree of stakeholder interaction that the workforce is involved in, typically expressed in terms of a percentage of total work hours. Stakeholders include customers, suppliers, distributors, investors, and employees. Stakeholder interactions are usually a good proxy for a critical business metric such as customer satisfaction or revenues. It should be noted that in some cases, this interaction may not take place with a human being. For instance, a field technician performing maintenance on transmission lines operated by a utility company may have no direct interaction with customers but may still be considered to be interacting with them indirectly.

## Information Requirement

Information requirement is the depth of information needed by a worker to complete the tasks involved in the business process. This information can range from the most basic (such as a work order number) to fairly complex (such as work order number, customer information, equipment warranty information, and parts inventory). It is not unusual for this information to be spread across multiple business functions (CRM, billing, dispatch, parts inventory, and so on), which affects the amount of integration required to gather the necessary data. Also the implications of the volume and richness of information must be taken into consideration. In some situations, simple pieces of information in high volumes may still require an end user to take some well-defined action.

### Time to Data

This is the degree to which the timeliness of data is important for the successful completion of the business process. Time to data refers to the real-time nature of the data required at the point of stakeholder interaction and is closely related to the information requirement dimension. It is highly important to assess the need for *real-time* access to information. In many situations, providing *right-time* access (where information is updated faster than the process's cycle) is sufficient to maintain the integrity of the business process. This distinction is especially critical since significant technical complexities (and associated risks and costs) are involved in providing real-time access to data.

### Process Maturity

This dimension captures the degree of maturity of the business process. This can range from low digitization (ad-hoc nature, paper-based, undocumented, inconsistent steps) to high digitization (well-defined, documented, completely automated, as in the case of electronic package routing and delivery). This dimension offers a glimpse into the potential inefficiencies and constraints of the current process. Unnecessary reliance on paper-based workflows usually correlates to a high error rate (due to transcription mistakes), redundant data entry, and longer cycle times for the process, which can eventually lead to higher costs. For example, writing medical prescriptions is a highly paper-based process that often leads to inefficiencies like follow-up calls from pharmacies to confirm instructions. In the worst cases, this process can result in major health complications or even fatalities.

Unlike the other dimensions, processes at any level of maturity can be good candidates for mobilization. A process with low maturity can benefit greatly, but may also require a considerable investment to mobilize. On the other hand, a more mature process can be relatively easy to mobilize, but it might not yield as many benefits. Interpreting this dimension depends in large part on how the process fits into an organization's overall mobility plan.

### *Business Process Dimension Questions*

The following questions are useful in capturing the location of a process within each dimension. Their answers build a better understanding of the business process and provide a data point for graphically mapping the process.

1. Workforce mobility: What percentage of the workforce associated with this process spends more than 40% of their time away from their desk?

   ☐ High: >60%

   ☐ Medium: 30-60%

   ☐ Low: <30%

2. Stakeholder interaction: What percentage of time does the mobile workforce (as identified in the previous item) spend interacting with stakeholders?

   ☐ High: >60%

   ☐ Medium: 30-60%

   ☐ Low: <30%

3. Information requirement: What kind of information does the mobile worker require to perform his or her daily tasks?

   ☐ High: More than three types of information, typically from different back-end applications (e.g., work order number, customer information, equipment warranty information, parts inventory)

   ☐ Medium: Typically no more than two or three components (e.g., customer contacts/address, product schematics)

   ☐ Low: One application or information source (e.g., email)

4. Time to data: How important is the timeliness of the data for successfully completing the business process?

   ☐ High: Process cannot move forward without access to real-time, updated information.

   ☐ Medium: Process can move ahead with slightly dated information (e.g., 24 hours old).

   ☐ Low: Process operates predominantly with static, relatively stable data.

5. Process maturity: How mature is the business process?

☐ High: Complete end-to-end process that is defined, documented, and highly digitized.

☐ Medium: Parts of the process are well defined and documented, and they are performed in a consistent manner. Some components are digitized, but the process still requires manual intervention or data entry into a system or application to proceed to the next step.

☐ Low: Process is not well defined or documented, and is usually performed in an ad-hoc manner. Process is completely manual/paper-based.

## A Sixth Dimension

Besides the five dimensions we discuss in this chapter, one other dimension applies to many business processes: the regulatory or liability requirements tied to the process or industry. By answering the following questions, you can get a sense of how mobility might enable stronger compliance:

1. Does this process need to comply with government mandates (e.g., public safety, worker safety, environmental regulation, or emergency preparedness)?

2. Do these mandates involve capturing and storing information for audit purposes?

3. Is the current mechanism used to capture and/or store information paper-based?

If you answer "yes" to all three questions, adding mobile elements like capturing information into a handheld mobile device the moment action is taken may well result in better compliance.

# Profiling Real-World Examples

To illustrate how this profiling technique works, we have chosen three examples:

- Nokia Networks field service equipment repair and return process

- Pharmaceutical sales process

- Utility company field force

Each example includes a description of the process before mobilization, an assessment based on the five dimensions, and a potential future state (that is, how the process might function with the mobile elements). We will return to these processes in Chapter 10 when we discuss how to build solid mobility business cases.

## Process 1: Nokia Networks Field Service Repair and Return Process

One of the business processes that was analyzed early on at Nokia was located in the Nokia Networks field service organization. This Nokia business group is a leading provider of network infrastructure, communications, and network platforms and services to operators and service providers. Within this organization, a team called CARE Hardware Services handles the repair and return process for hardware included in customer service contracts.

The typical sequence of activities in the original repair and return process used by Nokia Networks in Europe looked like this:

1. A field service engineer, often sharing a computer with other field service workers, would receive a work assignment at the office.

2. Upon receiving this information, the engineer would review the case to gather relevant information: site access details, parts information, site map and directions, special instructions, and so on.

3. If the parts needed for the repair were already in her van, the engineer would proceed directly to the site. If not, she would visit a satellite warehouse to acquire the appropriate parts before going to the customer site.

4. Upon arriving at the customer site, the engineer would replace the faulty item with a working part (either new or recycled).

5. The engineer would then write 1) the serial numbers of both the faulty and new parts and 2) a description of the problem on a paper copy of the failure report.

6. After attaching the barcode sticker from the failure report to the faulty part, the engineer would take the faulty part and the report back to the office.

7. All faulty parts would then be shipped to a centralized consolidation site in Europe, where they would be sent to any one of several repair vendors, depending on the specific part in question.

When viewed from the perspective of how mobile capabilities can improve this process, the following information is relevant:

• The workers in the organization (more than 2,000 Nokia employees and subcontractors) spent more than 40% of their time away from their desk.

• Dispatching workers involved little in the way of automated systems.

• The information that an engineer had to gather at the Nokia office before visiting a site involved a great deal of preparation.

• Phone calls to the Nokia office were required while the engineer was on-site to request additional information and to report on-site status.

• It was extremely difficult to combine preventive maintenance and emergency visits due to lack of knowledge about on-site equipment.

• Tracking repair parts at the site was almost completely paper-based.

• No accurate or updated status was available on the faulty parts from the time they left the customer site, were sent to the central consolidation site, and were delivered to the repair vendor.

• The process included numerous material re-routing and tracking steps.

We have used the business process profiling questions mentioned earlier to create a graphical representation of the Nokia Networks repair and return process (Figure 13).

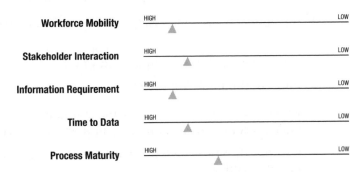

Figure 13. Profile of Nokia Networks repair and return process.

This profile reflects the high mobility rate of the field service engineers: they typically spend most of their time either in transit or at a customer site. It also reveals the heavily paper-oriented nature of the process, and the potential for inefficiencies due to errors, transcription problems, dual data entry, and so forth. Finally, it indicates that, to complete their jobs successfully, the engineers need access to data that must be frequently gathered from a variety of back-end applications. When charted together on a profile diagram, these factors indicate that the process is a potential candidate for mobilization.

It turns out that separating the physical return of the faulty part from the associated information (problem ticket number, repair vendor information, part numbers, tracking details, and so on) reduces slack in the process in the following ways:

- The field service engineer no longer needed to be in a specific location to receive and report on work assignments.

- The return process could be initiated without waiting for the field service engineer to be in a specific location (i.e., back at the Nokia office).

The following high-level solution addresses some of the key shortcomings mentioned above by adding mobile capabilities to the repair and return process:

- Equip the field service engineer with a mobile device, a barcode scanner, and a portable printer.

- Require the field service engineer to use the mobile device to receive and report on work assignments.

- Package information relevant to the case in the work assignment and make it available on the mobile device.

In the new process, the engineer arrives at the customer site and carries out the following tasks:

- Log arrival time on the mobile device.

- Replace the faulty part with a new part.

- Use the barcode scanner to read the part numbers for the faulty part and the new part into the mobile device.

- Capture the Air Way Bill number into an application on the mobile device.*

- Use the application to retrieve the repair vendor's address from a database that is also located on the mobile device.*

- Print a sticker with all relevant information using the portable printer.

- Attach the sticker to the faulty item.

- Update the work assignment on the mobile device, which initiates multiple messages to internal and external systems, including a third-party logistics service provider (LSP) and Nokia's SAP system.

* This information is provided by an LSP. It eliminates the need for a paper-based failure report and its subsequent handling.

After leaving the customer site, the engineer drops the faulty part at the nearest LSP pickup facility, where it is delivered directly to the correct repair vendor, thus bypassing consolidation, interim warehousing, and logistics processing.

Separating information flow from the physical and temporal dimensions of a business process—location, time, goods—lets you tease out.

## Process 2: Pharmaceutical Sales Process

The pharmaceutical industry is one of the most competitive in the world. Organizations rely on their sales forces to capitalize on multi-billion dollar drug development budgets and to increase revenues and retain market share before patents expire and generic drugs start eating away at revenues and profit margins. A typical big pharma company spends approximately 25-30% of its annual revenue on sales and marketing, relying on its sales force to build direct relationships with physicians to drive product sales.

The effectiveness of the direct sales force is critical for leveraging the maximum potential of each drug before it loses patent protection. However, these "feet on the street" must cope with the following difficulties:

- Diminishing face time with physicians

- Long downtimes (while driving to appointments or sitting in a physician's waiting room)

- Lack of timely access to information (product brochures, clinical information, drug interactions, research briefs, etc.)

- Lack of flexibility in scheduling (dealing with cancelled meetings, setting up visits if in close proximity and within window of a scheduled follow-up, etc.)

- Sample management regulations (required by the Food and Drug Administration in the United States)

- Coordination with other team members visiting the same physician

- Data entry into corporate CRM or sales force automation (SFA) systems as mandated by the sales management team

In an environment where a slight slip in the daily appointment schedule with physicians can trigger a disproportionately large negative impact on sales, sales managers need visibility into the performance of their sales force on a daily basis. This is the only way for them to identify problems and make adjustments before it is too late. Applying the business process profiling technique to the pharmaceutical sales process produces the profile shown in Figure 14.

Figure 14. Profile of a pharmaceutical sales process.

This profile reflects a process with a highly mobile workforce that has a very high degree of interaction with a key stakeholder community (physicians). Effective interaction with physicians depends on the sales force having timely access to a variety of information—sometimes in the middle of a meeting with a physician. The requirement for information is bidirectional in nature: from the corporate office to the field and vice versa. Much of this information exchange is not as automated as it could be—sales people typically write their notes on paper and then transcribe them into a CRM or SFA application at the end of the day.

The brief assessment of this process indicates a strong potential for improvement by adding mobile elements. For example, equipped with a mobile device that has appropriate access to corporate information, a salesperson's daily schedule might look like this:

06:30     Day begins. Download the following to mobile device: schedule, important announcements, reminders, alerts, quota updates, etc.

06:40     Review downloaded information and initiate appropriate action.

08:50     Proceed to first scheduled meeting.

09:30     Use downtime spent waiting in a physician's office as follows:

- Review latest product and competitive positioning to target message to physician.

- Request specific information from sales support team.

- Respond to email.

- Reschedule upcoming meetings due to changes requested via email by other physicians.

09:40        Pull up relevant research study to answer physician's question during meeting.

09:50        Provide samples to physician, obtain electronic signature from physician, and update sample management application.

10:00        Finish meeting, update meeting notes on mobile device, and possibly transmit notes to a CRM or SFA application.

10:00-17:00  Attend other meetings as scheduled, repeating the process outlined above.

17:00        End day with final transmission of meeting notes, rescheduling of meetings, and so on.

## Process 3: Utility Company Field Force

The utilities industry is one of the most critical components of any nation's infrastructure, and also an industry that ends up as a hot-button issue, especially as increased deregulation and the attendant pricing structures have brought it to the center of political debate in several industrialized nations.

Additionally, by virtue of its having geographically dispersed assets and being a major building block of any economy, the utilities industry has the potential of becoming the target of terrorism. The pressure on the industry to raise its emergency preparedness and response capabilities is immense, because such an attack could have significant human costs, not to mention a crippling effect on the economy.

In the United States, this industry is on the verge of a demographic shift in its field workforce: more than half of the field employees will be retiring within the next decade. The typical new employee is more technologically literate, but lacks experience and access to the tacit knowledge that the retiring employee possesses.

Running a top-notch field service organization in such a scenario is a key factor for the long-term competitiveness of a utility company. The field service organization is also critical to ensuring that the utility complies with regulatory agencies such as the Federal Energy Regulation Commission (FERC) and state public utilities commissions in the United States.

The field service organization of a typical utility company has to deal with a variety of problems, including the following:

- Multiple work types with varying priorities, service level agreements (SLAs), and skill set requirements (e.g., activities at or near customer locations; planned maintenance; and expansion or upgrade activities)

- Tacit knowledge, especially in the case of more seasoned workers, that compensates for incorrect or inaccurate work order assignments or incorrect associated information

- Downtime management (time spent in transit and idle time)

- Accurate tracking and reporting of work performed across the organization

- Complex scheduling and dispatching

Evaluating this process as a potential candidate for mobilization by applying the profiling technique described earlier results in the following profile (Figure 15):

Figure 15. Profile of a utility company field force.

As with the pharmaceutical example, the utilities industry field force is highly mobile. The success of both groups is predominantly a result of providing the right information to the right worker. In the case of the utilities industry, this means assigning a work order to the most suitable worker, ensuring a complete and correct work order, and providing accurate safety information and relevant documentation. Once the work order is completed, it is also essential that the correct details are entered in the appropriate back-end systems in a timely manner. Moving away from paper-based processes—using a clipboard to document activities—can save time and eliminate errors by reducing the need to transcribe information into a computer later.

After adding mobile elements to the utility field technician's job, the customer service process would look like this:

- A call to the utility's customer support hotline generates a work order.

- The work order is assigned to the most suitable worker using predefined algorithms for scheduling and dispatch.

- Upon receiving the work order, the technician travels to the site and performs the specified job.

- Once the job is completed, the technician updates the status using a handheld device and initiates an update to the appropriate back-end applications.

## Summary

Because mobility so often facilitates information exchange—which is a critical component of most business processes—it is very important to consider mobility from a business process perspective. As illustrated by the examples presented in this chapter, adding mobile elements to business processes makes information, applications, and communication channels available to workers in dramatically new ways. As we apply this perspective to our mobilization efforts at Nokia, we are beginning to see how mobility can help us stay competitive and capture new business opportunities.

# Things to Consider

Understanding your organization's business processes will help you identify where mobility can streamline processes and boost performance levels.

- Evaluating traditionally mobile parts of your organization (e.g., field services and sales forces) is a good place to start your efforts, but do not overlook the less obvious horizontal processes where adding mobile elements can create significant benefits. Which horizontal processes in your organization could benefit from mobilization?

- Who are the major business process owners in your organization? How can you involve them in evaluating processes for mobilization?

- Follow the clipboard: paper-based processes are a good place to start identifying business processes as candidates for mobilization. That said, more mature (highly digitized) processes can also be good candidates for mobilization.

- When a process crosses organizational boundaries, how will you convince stakeholders of the benefits their organizational unit will receive from mobilizing the process? How will you help them justify their investment?

A mobilized business process should not involve any unusual activity on the part of the workforce. It should embed itself in the normal daily activities of the workforce as seamlessly as possible. Higher integration with daily activities results in better user adoption and likelihood of success for the business process mobilization.

- Consider the demographics (age, location, technical proficiency, union affiliation, etc.) of the workforce that will be affected by adding mobile elements to a business process. What effect, if any, will that have on your plans to mobilize the process?

- How will you address the "big brother" perception often associated with mobility (that it is about providing additional visibility or compliance information to managers)?

# 7
# Choosing Mobile Technology Enablers

*When you talk to users about mobile technology, you have to focus on real benefits—not jargon. You don't tell them about IMAP IDLE or Java MIDP 2.0—you show them how they can use their smartphone to read email, present slides, receive faxes, review and edit documents, surf the web, and access calendar and contact information. When you start to do all these things with your phone, it really becomes a trusted and valuable personal tool...an extension of yourself that helps you in all areas of life.*

*– Jyrki Rosenberg, Director of Strategic Marketing*
*Nokia Technology Platforms*

Most innovations that reshape our world start from the grassroots: someone finds a cool new PDA or a smartphone in a local gadget shop and brings it to work. The innovation is amazing, and everyone wants one. And pretty soon everyone has one. Oh, and by the way, it is useful. It makes us more efficient. It can even change how we do business, sometimes dramatically.

This chapter is not a comprehensive guide to choosing the tools and technologies that will guarantee a successful mobility initiative—there are other books that discuss that topic in detail. Our discussion of mobile technology comes from a business management perspective and focuses on the key *considerations* that business decision makers should be aware of when evaluating technologies that can enable greater mobility in their business. The intent is to offer the knowledge and experience Nokia has gained—sometimes the hard way—about mobile technologies. We leave the choice of specific technologies to the IT staff and leadership of each organization because they are more intimately aware of the company's needs, desired direction, and current level of technology.

As the mobility team considered how technology fit into Nokia's mobility plans, they had two major objectives:

- Leverage existing network infrastructure, hardware, and applications whenever possible (e.g., voice, email, databases, and authentication).

- Create an open and flexible environment that would adapt and grow with Nokia's business and mobile workforce.

The team cringed at the thought of ripping and replacing technology, knowing that not only was it an ineffective way to incorporate mobile capabilities, but it would also make selling their business cases much harder. The team was determined to make the fewest changes possible to Nokia's existing infrastructure, while also accounting for the costs of integration and training, and the availability of in-house support. To keep the IT environment flexible, the team decided that, whenever possible, the mobility infrastructure should be based on open standards and should avoid proprietary device designs. This approach would allow Nokia's workforce to choose from a variety of devices with the functionality and connection methods best suited to their job tasks.

When the team began to assess Nokia's existing infrastructure, they found it helpful to ask questions such as the following:

- How do we shape Nokia's business to take optimal advantage of innovative mobile technology—and what are the risks?

- How do we standardize, support, and synchronize innovative mobile tools?

- Does our existing email system meet our users' needs? Can it be mobilized? What is needed to mobilize it?

- How important is remote access to internal databases and data?

- Can users access internal applications, including custom-built applications and packages like SAP? How well do these internal systems integrate?

- What types of authentication processes need to be followed? Can existing directory and authentication systems like Active Directory and Radius work in mobile scenarios?

- What are the best methods of ensuring the security of company confidential information such as corporate contacts, email, business strategies, and sales forecast numbers?

As we mentioned earlier, the team knew that addressing the needs of the people, processes, and technology affected by the solution was vital to the overall success of Nokia's mobility initiatives (Figure 16).

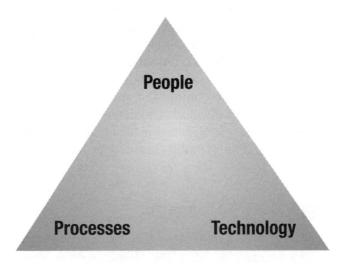

Figure 16. Crucial factors for successful mobility initiatives.

Experience had also taught the team that having the technology infrastructure in place early was a critical aspect of the transition to mobility, because it allowed the business processes and workforce to adapt to the changing environment more easily. In spite of this insight, the team was confronted with challenges that typically fell into one of two categories:

- Workforce expectations. Given the nature of some back-end systems, not all essential data and applications could be accessed remotely. Setting employee expectations about what they could and could not access remotely with mobile devices was crucial.

- Lack of industry standards. Because mobile technologies are still in early stages of development with few accepted industry standards, Nokia's IT administrators were sometimes hampered in their ability to implement mobile technologies. Even though industry standards groups are making strides to ensure that mobile software and hardware are effective, secure, and interoperable, the inconsistencies continue to be challenging.

Mobile technology in and of itself can be a challenge with such a wide range of options to choose from, including different wireless connectivity methods, mobile operating systems, and varying screen sizes and resolutions on mobile devices. Understandably, this can create uncertainty and doubt among business decision makers about whether to commit to a specific technology now or wait to see how things develop. The overriding challenge is determining whether the risk of delaying a decision outweighs the potential benefits of adding mobile capabilities now.

## Driving Industry Standards

Most people would agree that industry standards are a good thing—they remove the headache of making different proprietary systems work together. Although the standards around mobile technologies are still in their infancy, many standards organizations are working to ensure that mobile software and hardware are effective, secure, and interoperable. Nokia participates in many of these organizations, including the Open Mobile Alliance, the Liberty Alliance, the Mobile Industry Processor Interface, and the Java Community Interface.

To help organizations make that decision, we explore the following five technology enablers, or building blocks, that must be in place for a mobility initiative to be successful:

- Mobile devices

- Mobile device management

- Connectivity

- Tools and applications

○ Security

Figure 17 illustrates how these enablers fit into the overall technology infrastructure. Understanding the challenges, questions, and issues surrounding these enablers is critical to generating discussion among business decision makers about how to best move their organization toward mobility. Our goal in this chapter is to create that understanding by sharing Nokia's experience.

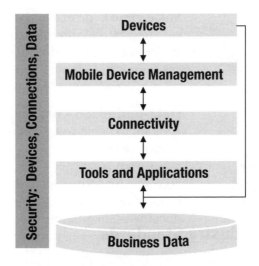

Figure 17. Five key mobile technology enablers.

# Mobile Devices

There is no one right mobile device for all workers—choosing the most suitable device depends on each person's work style and work tasks. For example, when a worker has to create a customer presentation heavy on graphics or manipulate a large spreadsheet, a laptop is the best mobile device. On the other hand, that same worker may prefer a smartphone with a keyboard for reviewing and replying to email while on the go.

Advances in mobile devices in recent years have created a wide range of choices that include the ability to use voice, data, barcode scanning, GPS, and RFID. In addition, many devices can capture signatures, video, and images. In the business environment, mobile devices are no longer just phones—they need to be managed as an IT resource.

Nokia has chosen to view mobile devices by using the following categorization:

 **Voice-centric devices:** These devices range from very basic mobile phones to smartphones that have significant data capacity but are still primarily voice communication tools.

 **Data-optimized communication devices:** In addition to being voice communication tools, these mobile devices are optimized for data use. They range from practically single-purpose devices (e.g., accessing mobile email) to devices that have a wide range of capabilities (e.g., accessing email, reviewing documents, interfacing with corporate applications, managing contact information). This category includes smartphones, wireless PDAs, and Communicators.

 **Data-centric devices:** This category primarily includes laptops and Tablet PCs, which are optimized for storing, viewing, and manipulating data, but usually lack mobile voice communication capabilities.

Each additional mobile device supported by a company's IT group increases the cost of support. Therefore, companies should clearly define a narrow list of supported mobile devices, keeping in mind that most devices usually last for about two years. When selecting mobile devices, a variety of human factors affect the choice:

- Most people want a single device that meets their mobile needs and, while they may want a keyboard, they probably do not want to use two hands to read email or answer a voice call.

- Special interfaces may require special training; if it seems too difficult, many people will just give up.

- People want to carry the device easily—discreetly in a purse or pocket, or on a belt for easy access.

- Many people see the type of mobile device they use as a status symbol.

Defining user communities based on mobility patterns and then selecting recommended toolsets for each community is a good practice for matching mobile devices with needs. This also guides people toward choosing appropriate tools that support them in their work tasks.

The following table lists some of the more technical factors to be considered when creating a mobile device selection strategy:

| Factors | Considerations |
| --- | --- |
| Who will use the device? | Sales, executives, field force, etc. |
| Where will the device be used? | In the office, at the airport, in the field, etc. |
| What is the purpose of the device and the scope of the applications to be used on it? | Single application such as email or a specific application like inventory management.<br><br>Multiple applications that access business resources such as the company intranet, collaboration tools, messaging, etc. |
| Define the device elements. | Device form factors (smartphone, PDA, flip, etc.).<br><br>Does the device have a camera? (Due to potential confidentiality issues, many organizations do not allow camera phones in their corporate environment.)<br><br>Is the device suitable for the environment in which it will be used (e.g., water resistant)?<br><br>What customization is available? Can the device be changed or configured based on the task or user needs?<br><br>What is the device's typical battery life?<br><br>What operating systems are supported (Symbian, PocketPC, Palm)? Can applications be added?<br><br>Is a backup utility (to PC or other media) available?<br><br>Does the device meet security and support requirements such as firewall and virus protection? |
| Who will the wireless carriers be? | Define carriers for data and voice services.<br>Optimize service cost through negotiations. |
| What corporate options will the carriers offer? | Roaming capabilities<br>Bandwidth<br>Speed, quality, and reliability<br>Text messaging |

Mobile devices are the crux of the mobile technology infrastructure. Having the right device makes a world of difference in terms of ease of use and user acceptance of mobile work habits.

## Convergent Technology

Demand for handheld wireless devices that can operate as both mobile phones and computers (convergent technology) is growing exponentially as organizations increasingly demand "everywhere" business communications devices. As a result, convergent devices such as smartphones and mobile PDAs are rapidly gaining presence in the business world, and wireless data services are gaining greater acceptance as well.

# Mobile Device Management

To improve the user experience and enable streamlined IT support, companies must develop mobile device management processes such as troubleshooting, installing software remotely, updating applications, and backing up and securing data on a mobile device. However, supporting mobile devices, which are often hundreds of miles from the nearest support services, can become very labor intensive and costly. To offset this problem, organizations should consider the following strategies for mobile device management:

- Provision the device. Ensure that mobile devices have the right capabilities and settings before they are deployed. Mobility infrastructures should include configuration plans that let IT consistently support mobile devices.

- Deliver services. Push new applications to the device once it is active and in service. Settings management, remote software distribution, inventory management, and device auditing are critical to remotely delivering services and providing a good user experience.

- Support mobile devices. Resolve technical and usability problems, and ensure data security. Train IT staff to support multiple devices on site and remotely.

Depending on the organization, it might make sense to treat mobile devices as IT resources. If that is the case, the IT department will play a major role—perhaps even the leading role—in deciding what mobile devices to select and how to manage them. The questions answered during the mobile device selection process will provide guidelines for developing the best possible device management practices.

> At Nokia, mobile devices are treated as IT resources: they are provisioned with a standard configuration and are managed and supported by IT staff.

# Connectivity

Mobility skeptics at Nokia pointed out that mobile networks do not always work as well as they do in the metropolitan Helsinki area where Nokia is headquartered. Addressing connectivity issues early—for example, access to quality wireless networks, offline scenarios for mobile workers, and the overarching issue of connection security (discussed later in this chapter)—will help ensure the success of a mobility initiative.

## Choosing Mobile Network Carriers

Choosing the best mobile network carrier for voice and data communications is essential. Generally, no single carrier provides the perfect fit for every mobile aspect of an organization. This means that many organizations will probably use different carriers for different regions as well as for different user communities. The choice of carrier depends on the community's degree of mobility (both inside and outside the corporate office), its typical hardware and application use (with associated bandwidth requirements), and the amount of collaboration and teamwork inherent in its work processes (Figure 18).

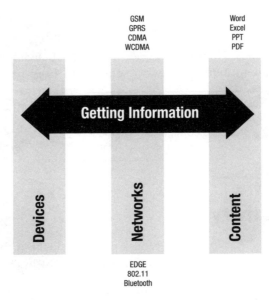

Figure 18. Mobile network and data transmission protocol options.

Most mobile carriers support General Packet Radio Service (GPRS) for mobile connections, and third-generation (3G) networks are also increasingly common. When mobile workers have to connect in different countries, they will often need to change the connection settings on their mobile devices. To facilitate mobile work, IT departments may find it useful to provide instructions for how to connect in various situations. With the advent of mobile devices that seamlessly roam between carriers and networks, workers will not be distracted by the need to reconfigure their devices, thus allowing them to focus on more productive activities.

## Making Mobile Connections

Being able to connect to corporate information networks from any place and at any time is at the heart of mobility. Mobile workers should be able to make connections in several ways, depending on their location, the device they are using (e.g., a smartphone or a laptop), and the available connection (WLAN, broadband, SSL VPN, mobile network, etc.). Figure 19 illustrates the different ways that mobile workers should be able to connect to corporate networks.

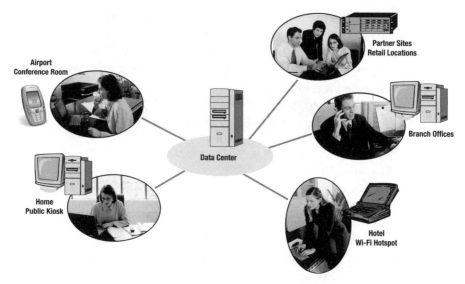

Figure 19. Mobile connection methods.

The software necessary for making these types of mobile connections should be installed on each company-provided mobile device. The rest of this section describes the different locations and types of mobile connections.

### Internal Wireless Local Area Network

Should an internal WLAN be an extension of the internal network or an extension of the network perimeter? An extension of the internal network may initially provide easier intranet access to mobile workers. In the future, however, an extension of the network perimeter may allow roaming between the internal WLAN and external mobile networks. A WLAN should not be seen as just an extension of the LAN—it should be considered as part of the mobility plan.

### General IP Access

Nokia provides virtual private network (VPN) gateway locations globally. Mobile workers have a user account and a VPN client on their mobile devices that let them access any of the VPN gateways, which in turn provide secure access to the internal corporate network over the public internet.

Nokia also uses a corporate-wide WLAN that covers our larger office locations. All WLANs offer similar service—allowing access to regional gateways located in the external network. This arrangement sets the stage for roaming between the corporate WLAN and external service provider networks such as GPRS, 3G, and Code Division Multiple Access (CDMA).

### Multiradio

Multiradio, a new capability that integrates multiple radio technologies in a single mobile device, allows mobile workers to connect to different kinds of wireless networks without having to spend time reconfiguring their devices. This capability will cover the following wireless access methods:

- Wide-area cellular technologies including Wideband Code Division Multiple Access (WCDMA) and their future evolutions

- Local communications like WLAN

- Proximity technologies, including Bluetooth and Near Field Communication (NFC)

- One-to-many broadcast communications, including Digital Video Broadcast-Handheld (DVB-H)

As more mobile devices come equipped with multiradio support, mobile workers will be able to focus on high value-adding work tasks instead of worrying about how to connect to an available wireless network.

### Home Office Connections

Home offices should have a reliable internet connection suitable for the worker's role and the tasks performed. Since home offices will become part of the mobility infrastructure, it might be beneficial for corporate IT departments to have a clearly defined list of approved and supported hardware, software, and internet connection providers. This approach could be expanded to allow—or even require—employees to submit a service request to the IT department to order the necessary hardware, software, and internet connections for their home offices.

Nokia employees have found that broadband access at home gives them fast and secure remote access to the application and information services hosted on Nokia's intranet. While following corporate IT guidelines, they use commonly available internet service providers for home office access to corporate services. Organizations wanting to facilitate a mobile workforce will need to explore the most effective solutions for providing connectivity to their remote workers.

### Hotspots

Hotspot WLAN services are popping up in cafes, coffee shops, malls, restaurants, hotels, and airports around the globe, with more service providers emerging every day. These external WLANs can provide mobile workers with good places for a quick, high-speed data sync—whether they are at a local coffee shop or at the Frankfurt airport waiting for a connecting flight.

The level of security provided by VPNs, firewalls, and virus protection is extremely crucial for mobile workers connecting to the corporate network from a hotspot WLAN. While it is possible to configure a secure connection from a hotspot, negotiating connection options with these service providers creates a much better experience for mobile workers. Often the service providers are also willing to offer consolidated billing, which frees mobile workers from paying as they go with a credit card. In addition to providing easy, protected access to the internal network, this method gives insight into mobile connection costs, which is particularly important in a corporate environment. Ultimately, deciding how to handle hotspot WLAN connections may be a question of optimizing security and costs.

# Tools and Applications

Mobility tools and applications provide access to information on mobile devices, in turn enabling better decision making and higher levels of productivity. They range from simple voice communication to complex mobile inventory and ordering systems. In the following sections, we discuss the tools and applications most likely to be used in a business mobility infrastructure.

## Voice and Data Convergence

Mobile voice is probably the archetypal mobility application. As voice and data networks converge, new technologies and offerings become key mobility enablers. Voice and data communication can potentially reduce operational costs and provide new productivity enablers. As Nokia has developed its mobility strategy, one important decision has been to bring voice and data network management under the same management umbrella. This has allowed us to develop new services and operations that take advantage of converging voice and data technologies.

### Voice Over IP

Nokia uses VoIP PBXs to route voice traffic to remote offices over internet connections wherever it makes financial sense. The strategy is to support and enhance mobility by using mobile devices. In addition, our fixed-to-mobile voice transition program removes the unnecessary duplication of an employee using both a fixed phone and a mobile phone, thus reducing overall costs and improving the ability to quickly contact employees.

### Voice and Web Conferencing

Conferencing technology is one of the most widely used mobile applications at Nokia. A key element of this technology is our global voice and web conferencing system, which can be accessed using local phone numbers that connect to Nokia's internal VoIP network. Employees use a VPN data connection for web conferencing as well as instant messaging, and can also use the connection to access voice conferencing via a web browser and VoIP.

## Email

After voice, email is the most popular communication medium in the business world. While it started out in many organizations as a privileged tool used almost exclusively by upper management, email has become a standard medium at all levels of an organization. Mobile workers are discovering that to be effective in their daily jobs, they increasingly require access to email from any location and at any time of the day (or night). To fulfill this need, mobile email has developed significantly over the past two years, and comes in two main varieties.

### Push and Pull Email

Push email allows messages, calendar updates, and meeting requests to be automatically delivered to workers' mobile devices via the wireless network. Changes in the mobile device's inbox are instantly mirrored in the desktop mailbox and vice versa. Pull email requires workers to request information from their mailbox. Most web-based email systems are of the pull variety.

Nokia has a long history of using mobile email through our internal, SMS-based Nokia One service. Mobile workers can use their mobile devices to receive notifications about important email messages when they arrive. This approach has minimized costs by not having to support multiple devices, and it has reduced the amount of equipment that mobile workers have to carry around. We are currently in the process of deploying a corporate-wide push email and personal information management (PIM) solution that will replace Nokia One. Push email provides significant benefits for improving worker productivity and email response times.

## Mobile Application Development

A common mobile technology challenge is figuring out how to get legacy and turn-key applications to interface with newer mobile technologies. Even with standards-based mobile technologies, integrating a legacy accounting application to deliver to or accept data from mobile devices can result in a variety of complications (for example, screen size and resolution, touch screen input, lack of QWERTY keyboard, and so on). Integrating with mobile devices may also increase the complexity of troubleshooting because there are more layers of technology infrastructure to deal with (device hardware, device operating system, application, wireless connectivity, and so on).

In a mobilized business, mobile devices need to connect to corporate database systems, application servers, and of course, the internet. Software development in such a connected environment may seem quite daunting, but development tools exist to ease the burden on software application developers. This section provides a high-level overview of some of the technologies and solutions available for application developers. We now consider the following facets of business software environments as they relate to mobile devices:

- Browser architecture
- Web Services
- Database
- Repurposing gateway

### Browser Architecture

As long as workers have network access, mobile browsers can connect them to data and forms. The gap between mobile and normal Web browsers continues to decrease—capabilities such as forms and frames can now be optimized for mobile devices, while Cascading Style Sheets (CSS) and Extensible Markup Language (XML) allow for separation of content and presentation. Because mobile browsers can display dynamic and static content based on a template structure while separating content from presentation, applications can send smaller amounts of data to mobile devices without sacrificing user experience or functionality.

### Web Services

Web Services are particularly well suited to mobile environments. Applications that use Web Services provide standard XML-based messaging interfaces, regardless of the platform on which the software application is running. All of this can facilitate software development where multiple operating platforms must co-exist. Several enterprise platforms exist for developing Web Service consumer and provider applications, and some of these have extensions for supporting mobile Web Service consumer development.

### Database

A database-driven solution can be built for small mobile devices by using a server-side proxy or by hosting a small database on the mobile device and synchronizing the data with corporate back-end systems. Local data storage can be implemented with currently available tools. Database clients are already available for this purpose, and there will be others in the future, all providing their own developer tools.

### Repurposing Gateway

Another option for providing direct web access from a mobile device to an application server is to use a repurposing gateway, which optimizes the content for different devices. These gateways identify the mobile device, analyze its display capabilities, and then compress files and reduce image resolution as required. In addition to reducing overall bandwidth requirements, this approach saves time and lowers data transmission costs.

A disadvantage of using a repurposing gateway is that it increases architectural complexity by adding another gateway and content transformation between the device and the application. Some content could be lost if the gateway is unable to process certain items. The performance is only as good as the gateway.

High-end mobile devices are expected to have adequate processing, storage, data transfer, and browsing capabilities to access most data directly. Nevertheless, repurposing gateways are a good alternative for delivering content to low-end devices with small screens, and for viewing large attachments over slow connections.

# Security

Security is the last and possibly the most important mobile technology enabler. In a mobilized business, sensitive information is handled and stored outside of the secure corporate premises. And as technology evolves, so does the task of securing sensitive information. Security must be a top priority in supporting mobile workers—without proper policies, training, and enforcement, security breaches will undoubtedly occur. Mobile workers need to be aware of security issues and know how to keep their data and devices secure.

A mobile security strategy should provide a secure data transmission platform and layer applications and other functionality onto that platform. It should consider the security of data in transit through a variety of networks and airspace. And perhaps most importantly, it should train mobile workers in proper information-handling procedures.

Technology provides a large part of the answer to overcoming security challenges: device security through remote locking messages, connection security through virtual private networks, and data protection through encryption and password protection are all options in a security strategy. This section discusses the following security issues:

- Device security

- Connection security

- Application security

## Device Security

Many of us have experienced it: you are at a restaurant or in a taxi and accidentally misplace your phone or PDA. Sometimes you are lucky enough to recover it, but often that is not the case. Because mobile devices leave the corporate premises, they have to be secured. Lost, stolen, or virus-compromised devices can have devastating results—corporate espionage is a real and significant risk.

The risk of corporate information being exposed when a mobile device is lost or stolen can be minimized by considering the following security precautions when building a mobile device security strategy:

- Password-protect mobile devices. If a device ends up in the wrong hands, a device password is the first line of defense. Strong passwords are essential: PIN codes and alphanumeric passwords of at least six characters should be used whenever possible.

- Incorporate data encryption on mobile devices. Unencrypted data can be retrieved easily from a lost or stolen device.

- Install software for remote data wiping. Establish a firm policy that a lost or stolen mobile device must be reported immediately to the proper department and to the carrier for immediate deactivation. With remote wiping and/or disabling software loaded on a missing device, corporate data can be wiped or locked, which would typically cause the person who stole the device to throw it away or try to reset it (which, in the case of locked data, would wipe out the data altogether).

- Establish a mobile device backup policy. If a device is lost or stolen, data backups on external media, such as Multimedia Memory Cards (MMC) or SecureDigital (SD) memory cards, are vital to restoring information.

- Constantly evaluate virus protection for mobile devices. Many desktop and laptop antivirus vendors offer virus protection for mobile devices. As mobility moves into the mainstream, it is only a matter of time before viruses, trojans, worms, and other malicious code target mobile devices. If mobile workers use public networks such as hotspot WLANs, it is especially important to use antivirus software and a firewall.

- Consider hardware-level security. When evaluating mobile devices for use with business applications, consider whether they provide security options at the hardware level (e.g., the ability to turn on and off functions like the camera or Bluetooth radio).

At Nokia, we use remote locking technology to render mobile devices unusable the moment they receive a pre-defined text message. This system has proven itself in the field. For example, a Nokia 9300 smartphone was stolen from a Nokia manager during his morning metro commute. He noticed the theft within a couple of minutes, and quickly contacted the help desk. The lock code was sent to the phone, making it unusable. The phone was later found in a trash bin outside the next metro station. Employing security procedures like these can reduce device security risks.

## Non-Approved Mobile Devices

Workers are often tempted to bring in their own mobile devices—personal devices that often conflict with corporate IT structure and policy. If they have administrative rights—as many knowledge workers and laptops users do—they may connect the device to their company-issued computer using synchronization software that came with the device. At that point, they can easily save incredibly sensitive corporate information on their personal devices. If the company is not ready to set and enforce a mobile device policy, the costs and risks associated with non-approved devices could quickly spiral out of control.

To protect both employees and corporate information, a mobile device policy should include provisions like the following for personal devices:

- If employees want to use personal mobile devices to access corporate applications or data, they must contact the IT department for approval. This also practice also allows the IT department to build an inventory of devices that are being used throughout the company.

- Employees must be educated about the risks involved in bringing in personal devices. Mobile device users must understand the following:

  - Data is almost never encrypted on these mobile devices— losing them could mean a major security breach.

  - Backups are rarely done, and loss of data could be disastrous.

  - Help desk support is usually unavailable for these mobile devices.

## Connection Security

Like conventional VPNs, mobile VPNs take advantage of internet connectivity to provide encryption and authentication, addressing the lack of security on the open internet. Mobile workers can establish IPSec VPN tunnels from their handheld devices to an IPSec gateway using any IP-based connection (such as WLAN or GPRS). The VPN tunnel lets mobile workers connect securely to the corporate network and access internal information and applications.

## Application Security

The applications mobile workers use also pose security risks. Organizations must ensure security, maintain trust, and protect mobile workers while providing them with useful and well-designed applications.

Creating a tiered access rights model—less strict for non-critical applications, more strict for confidential information and applications—addresses security needs across the board. It ensures that applications and information are available to mobile workers based on the degree of authentication and type of access method.

For example, each of the following could allow a different degree of access to corporate applications and information:

- User authentication to corporate authentication servers

- Encrypted connection established from mobile device to corporate system via Secure Sockets Layer (SSL) or VPN

- Mobile device meets requirements such as installed and updated antivirus software, VPN client, SSL-capable browser, corporate application, correct configuration, and other security criteria

Ultimately, it becomes necessary to balance security with ease of use. If the security is too cumbersome, it may prevent users from realizing the potential business benefit. On the other hand, if the policy is too loose, the organization runs major security risks. For example, when Nokia introduced its new Communicator, the adoption rate for the built-in mobile email client was low. People seemed to prefer the text message-based Nokia One email service—even though its email capabilities were very limited.

When users were asked why they were reluctant to switch to an application with better functionality, they pointed to Nokia's security policy. It required strong authentication and was consequently perceived as cumbersome (it required a separate authentication using a SecureID card) and time consuming (users had to re-authenticate each time the data connection went down). In contrast, when Nokia piloted its push email technology with internal groups, use of all other mobile email options dropped to almost zero. Why? According to users, the secure authentication method was much easier to use.

Finally, all security features should be considered as a whole: encryption, remote data wiping, device authentication, device policy enforcement, and so on. These features should be addressed together—no single feature provides the needed protection without the others.

# Things to Consider

- What existing technologies can you leverage in your mobility initiatives? How can doing this save time and money?

- Consider the type of device that would best suit the needs of your business. Base your selection on users, purpose, form factor, and availability.

- How will you manage a mobile solution once it has been deployed? Consider how you would remotely manipulate and update the mobile devices once they are in the field. In addition, what help desk skills must be acquired to support your mobile workers?

- How will mobile workers connect to your organization's network? Public hotspots and private wireless access points provide high-speed access for many mobile devices, but you must also consider data encryption, device firewalls, and antivirus issues.

- Assess which mobile carriers provide the best coverage in your operating areas. Consider the monthly costs of voice and data offerings.

- How will your organization provide home office workers with high-speed internet and VPN access to business resources?

- Think about how your voice strategy could support mobile ways of working. How could you avoid double infrastructure and support costs (on both fixed and mobile voice services)?

- Conferencing is one of the "quick wins" provided by mobility. How will you ensure cost-effective mobile access to voice and data conferencing services?

- Consider mobilizing email first—this solution almost always results in immediate success.

- Which applications could you mobilize after email? What would be the best way to mobilize applications (browser, database, etc.)?

- Most importantly, how will you provide security for your newly mobilized business? Consider all aspects of device, connection, and application security. You need to develop policies around VPN, virus protection, data encryption, device disablement, and tiered access, while at the same time ensuring that your security measures do not impede functionality to the point of making mobile applications unusable.

# 8

# Optimizing the Mobile Workplace

*Remote connectivity, mobile devices, and working across time zones are creating a new paradigm where people can work practically anywhere—at home, in cafes and airports, in taxis, and even at the park. We've found that on average, people spend less than half of their working time sitting at a desk. This challenges businesses to rethink how to make "place" really perform. The secret lies in recognizing and supporting emerging work practices. We have to provide a variety of places for collaborative and individual work, both in the office and beyond. Combining the choice of place with available technology, personnel policies, and team dynamics that embrace a "work anywhere" culture lets us truly support the new mobile work paradigm.*

—*Bethany Davis, Director, Workplace Solutions*
*Nokia Human Resources*

In the first half of 2005, Nokia had an average of 7,000 active mobile email users, 44,000 laptop users with remote connection capability, and at least one mobile phone per employee. In addition to that, the company's employees made an average of 580,000 remote connections per month to Nokia's network. These figures reflect a substantial amount of work taking place outside the traditional corporate office premises. So what kind of impact has mobility had on the workplace at Nokia?

Like most organizations, Nokia has a corporate real estate and facilities group that plans and manages its office space. And like most organizations, workplace planning at Nokia was in large part determined by traditional thought about space—enclosed or open spaces based on status and team dynamics. The efforts to mobilize Nokia's business prompted the mobility team to take an in-depth look at the reality of how that space was being used. That closer look revealed the following:

- A typical desk at a Nokia corporate office is occupied less than 50% of the time.

- Meeting rooms are in very high demand (which explains, at least partly, why people are not at their desks).

- Working in remote and distributed teams has led people to shift their work hours to overlap with team members in different time zones.

- The rise of high-bandwidth connectivity at home is allowing many people to work occasionally from home—even without formal home-working policies.

Interestingly, many of these changes happened before Nokia began its formal efforts to build a mobile business, indicating that the shift to mobile work habits was already underway. The team knew from prior investigations into employee work styles that different user communities had different levels of mobility (see Chapter 5). Similarly, some employees felt that they had more choice in where or when to work than others based on either personal circumstances or work task requirements. However, the overriding sentiment was that Nokia's employees were looking for more choice and flexibility in where to work. This chapter introduces some of the changes that Nokia has made to make "place" perform for its employees.

A study at Nokia's headquarters in Espoo, Finland, found that at any given moment, only 40% of employees were at their dedicated workstations, with the average being closer to 30%.

# What Is Place?

When employees have tools and policies that allow them to work where they feel most productive, they begin to expand their definition of the workplace. Rather than thinking of the office as the only place where work happens (a common mindset developed over years of office work), employees with mobile tools begin to take advantage of an entire network of places, each with particular characteristics that suit different tasks or needs at different times (Figure 20).

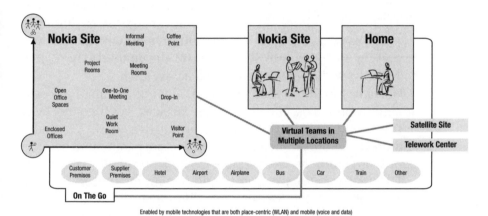

Enabled by mobile technologies that are both place-centric (WLAN) and mobile (voice and data)

Figure 20. Working in multiple places.

This network of places can be divided into two main groups:

1. Public places (airports, taxis, parks, and so on), and locations over which Nokia has only minor influence (home offices, selected partner hotels or conference settings, and in some cases partner sites)

2. Places designed and maintained by Nokia (for example, an employee's primary office, as well as other Nokia locations)

If we look at these places more closely, it becomes apparent that different solution sets are needed to enable work in each type of place.

# Working in Public and Low Influence Places

Major airports, hotels, and other public venues are increasingly providing WLAN hotspots, while public internet connections are becoming available in even more locations. WLAN, GPRS access, and the ever-increasing possibilities of 3G-roaming can turn a hotel lobby or sidewalk cafe into a functional workplace where mobile workers can participate in a conference call, share a presentation, review a report, or check their email. In a traditional work environment, employees would have to be at their desks or reserve a conference room to get this work done. In contrast, mobility allows employees to take advantage of traditionally unproductive downtime—while waiting in the hotel lobby to join colleagues for dinner or taking a taxi across town.

> Working in public with a smaller mobile device increases control over who can view the screen.

Nokia has found that its influence on work in public places is limited to providing effective mobile devices, good connectivity options, and policies for secure, productive work. Of these, appropriate information security behaviors are paramount, because *people* are often the weakest link in an organization's security.

The freedom to work virtually anywhere carries a heavy responsibility. Mobile workers must be especially aware of their work *behaviors* and take care to not compromise company security or inadvertently reveal classified information to a competitor having lunch at the next table. Authorized procedures for working outside corporate premises should be issued by the corporate security department, and all employees, but particularly mobile workers, need to be properly educated about those policies.

Security policies for a mobile workforce should include best practices such as the following:

- Always use reliable, secure authentication.

- Use a secure access method like VPN or SSL to establish remote connections to the corporate network.

- Take extra precautions when talking in public places. Loud discussions on the phone or in person should be avoided—especially in crowded areas.

- Whenever possible, make business calls in an isolated area. Sensitive issues should not be discussed in an uncontrolled environment.

- Mobile workers should familiarize themselves with information classification guidelines and never leave documents unattended regardless of their classification.

- Mobile workers should take all company-related documents with them when they leave a non-company location. All unnecessary documents should be shredded before being thrown away.

- Never leave mobile devices (including laptops), documents, or other belongings unattended. This equipment should be transported as carry-on luggage.

- Use privacy filters on laptop screens when working in external premises. Use pin-codes, screen locks, and other available security features in mobile devices.

- Do not allow family members or other individuals to use corporate equipment. Do not transfer any information from corporate to home equipment or vice versa.

- In the case of a work-related incident (e.g., accident, lost equipment or work-related documents), mobile workers should report the incident immediately to their managers and any other relevant parties.

Working away from a corporate site requires more precautions than working on corporate premises. Even though external connections are usually easy to establish at an airport lounge or in a cafe, it is crucial to maintain the absolute confidentiality of information. Mobile workers must understand that they are responsible for the confidentiality of all information in their possession, regardless of where they work.

## Road Office Toolkit

Over the years, Nokia's road warriors have given feedback about the basic set of tools that helps them stay productive while on the move. The following checklist is a good starting point for mobile workers who are new to travel.

- Mobile charger that works on the airplane and in a car
- Charged extra battery for each mobile device
- Privacy filter and lock for laptop
- International AC adaptor pack
- Modem and AC surge protector
- Retractable phone and LAN cables
- Noise-canceling headset and/or ear plugs
- Hardcopy of important phone numbers, including credit card companies, travel agency, corporate help desk, and so on
- Neck pillow and sleep mask

# Working at Home

Telecommuting from home has become increasingly common, with some companies even incorporating the practice into their business model. As a result, organizations are beginning to develop guidelines and offer advice about setting up and using home workspace. For example, they may provide a suggested list of furniture and equipment for employees who work from home to improve work efficiency.

Nokia only has few employees who use their home office as a primary work setting, so we do not typically provide home office furniture. However, we have developed the following guidelines on how to set up a productive workspace for employees who periodically choose to work from home:

- A home workspace should be a quiet area separated from the rest of the house. If this is not possible, we do not recommend working from home.

- The workspace should be well lit and adequately ventilated.

- Ergonomics should meet corporate occupational health recommendations.

- Proper technical solutions that enable remote working must be available (e.g., electrical outlets, access to the internet, etc.).

The security procedures that apply to working outside the office also apply to working at home (privacy during telephone conversations, a safe for storing sensitive information, and a shredder for destroying documents, and so on).

# Working at Nokia Locations

The places that Nokia can influence the most are, of course, its own offices. Our corporate workspace has been designed for decades based on the traditional assumption that people come to the office every day to do their work. Their team members and co-workers are located at the same site, as close to them as possible to enable efficient cooperation and interaction. However, with the advent of mobile work habits, Nokia began to rethink the design and management of its corporate workspaces.

Mobility does not change the corporate office environment per se. It is quite possible to continue working in the office in much the same way as before. The greatest visible change mobility brings to the office is that fewer people are around since many are working at other locations.

However, if a company is willing to look beyond the traditional workspace model, mobility can act as an enabler to a revised use of office space. WLAN, mobile voice, and a variety of shared settings—including open space, quiet rooms, meeting rooms, project team rooms, drop-in space, and informal places—create a flexible work environment that supports many different tasks.

## Making Place Perform with FlexiSpace

Over time, Nokia has developed a concept referred to as FlexiSpace to support mobile work habits at its corporate facilities. At its heart, FlexiSpace is about creating a combination of flexible spaces that people can choose as their work requirements change. This concept replaces the traditional idea of workplace where each person's desk or office is his or her home base.

In its simplest terms, FlexiSpace re-evaluates and reassigns space in the corporate facility, making it available for use on an as-needed basis to support work tasks. Some of its principal characteristics are as follows:

- Depending on patterns of workspace occupancy, some people have assigned workplaces while others do not. This allows elasticity in group sizes and easily accommodates short-term growth and change.

- More teaming and interactive spaces are available, providing a stronger focus on knowledge sharing and communication.

- More informal layouts and movable elements foster creativity and self-expression.

- Spaces include interactive and quiet spots to serve different work needs.

FlexiSpace requires organizations to rethink traditional work patterns and  be willing to experiment with new mobile work practices. Potential changes include the following:

- Relying less on physical resources (such as paper files) and more on technology to allow "anywhere" access

- Taking an active approach to deciding what type of space best suits each activity—thinking of the entire mix of spaces as available for use instead of only a single workspace

- Recognizing and encouraging differing patterns of mobility for different work functions and personal styles

- Balancing the needs of the team with the needs of the individual when deciding on work locations

> An early FlexiSpace pilot showed that an organization with 2,000 employees could save as much as 30% in annual real estate costs by moving to a more flexible space allocation model.

Because Nokia's workforce had already begun to incorporate mobile work practices, we have pursued the FlexiSpace model with great interest. The rest of this section discusses key aspects of the FlexiSpace model.

## Shifting to More Collaborative Spaces

The easiest tasks to achieve in a mobile work mode are individual and independent. Workers do not depend on another person's schedule to get these kinds of tasks done, and individual work also places fewer demands on the work space than do conversations or meetings. Interestingly, while people often do individual work in the office, their choice to come to the office is primarily triggered by the desire to be with other people, whether for formal meetings or the informal social interaction inherent in an office setting.

As a result, Nokia's FlexiSpace workspaces include many interactive settings for small groups of two to four people. Why the focus on small groups? In Nokia's traditional offices, small groups frequently reserved larger meeting rooms designed for 10-12 people because these rooms were equipped with data projectors. Now, smaller meeting rooms are being equipped with projectors or flat panel displays to accommodate the need for small groups of people to work collaboratively on documents or presentations. In many cases, remote team members participate in these activities, so virtual collaboration software is also used. This approach removes the need to huddle around a tiny laptop screen. It also frees larger meeting rooms for larger groups of people.

In addition to meeting rooms, which are often thought of as *the* interactive space, Nokia is also emphasizing the value of informal interactive spaces in its FlexiSpace locations. For a highly mobile worker, one of the benefits of being in the office is seeing and being seen by colleagues. Of course, in a highly mobile workforce, there is no guarantee that colleagues will be in the office at the same time. However, we have observed that teams are scheduling periodic meetings in the office and are taking advantage of free time during planned events to meet informally. Nokia employees tend to have collegial networks that cross many sites, so it is not uncommon to see colleagues from two different locations running into one another in the cafeteria or cafe and saying, "I didn't know you'd be here today!" Providing places where people can spontaneously interact is increasingly important.

> Don't go into hiding. "Out of sight" can easily become "out of mind." Make an extra effort to maintain your social networks at work.

## Going Wireless—Every Place Is a Workspace

Remember when employees from out-of-town would wander through the office searching for a free LAN cable to get connected to the network? Thanks to wireless connectivity, almost any place can become a short-term workspace. At Nokia, employees are finding that corporate cafeterias and cafes can be great places to finish a few emails or to polish a slide presentation while having a quick cup of coffee. With WLANs and mobile devices, the same kind of connectivity that employees use in public places can also be used in the corporate office.

## From "My Desk" to "My Neighborhood"

Having an assigned desk at a corporate office makes it easy to establish a sense of belonging. In the past, many consulting and sales organizations adopted concepts such as "hot desking" or "hoteling" to respond to a mobile workforce, but the perception of sterility and uniformity in these spaces has presented a challenge to adoption. It is a difficult balance: creating a sense of belonging in a space that cannot be personalized because it might be used by someone else the next day.

Nokia is still trying to work out the best way to handle personalization for mobile workers. But what we do know is that these workers value and desire a team base or neighborhood where their colleagues are likely to gravitate when they come to the corporate office. One of our approaches is to define the heart, or anchor point, of a neighborhood by locating non-mobile workers, shared resources, and storage spaces in one area. This allows teams to have a place where they can go and be close to the people they are most interested in seeing in the office, rather than wandering the entire floor looking for a place to sit. We are careful, however, to avoid defining the boundaries of these neighborhoods, because defining territories too precisely would decrease flexibility in how the space can be used.

# The Cost of Workspace

Regardless of whether an organization chooses to adopt a FlexiSpace model, it is good to understand the real cost of workspace. In most companies, real estate costs are the second largest expense after salaries, and these costs have a direct impact on the bottom line. The traditional workspace model can either be accepted as a cost of doing business, or it can be challenged in favor of a solution that reduces costs. The following table illustrates how FlexiSpace can be a factor in reducing the overall cost of doing business by maximizing the actual use of corporate office space. (Note that the figures are for illustrative purposes only.)

| Traditional Workspace Model | |
| --- | --- |
| A dedicated, single-user office + allocation for common space | 20 Sqm + 10 Sqm |
| Cost of space per month | €20.0 |
| Monthly cost for space | €600.0 |
| Average 18 working days per month* | 36 hours of usage |
| 2 hours of daily use** | = €16.67 / hour |

| FlexiSpace Model | |
| --- | --- |
| A dedicated, single-user office + allocation for common space | 20 Sqm + 10 Sqm |
| Cost of space per month | €20.0 |
| Monthly cost for space | €600.0 |
| Average 20 bookable days per month* | 160 hours of usage |
| 2 hours of daily use** | = €3.75 / hour |

* In the traditional model, employees are allocated 100% of the use of their assigned space, even though they may only use it for a small percentage of the allocated time. In the FlexiSpace model, several employees have access to a bookable space on an as-needed basis, resulting in maximum use of the space and lower hourly cost.

** Concentrated sessions, where having individual, quiet space is necessary.

# The Skeptics Speak

The move into a flexible office environment is not easy, and cultural issues need to be taken into account. Nokia faced the following two cultural difficulties:

- A century-long tradition of work areas that reflected status (e.g., corner offices with the best view and amount of space allocated by seniority)

- A company culture that emphasized a strong team mentality, with employees accustomed to working in close proximity in a highly networked setting

FlexiSpace skeptics raised a number of concerns. In the following table, we present those concerns together with a related benefit and a suggestion for handling the concern.

| Benefit of FlexiSpace | Skeptic's concern | Addressing concern |
|---|---|---|
| The company saves money in real estate, allowing investment in other resources. | "The company is losing money because I am less productive." | In many cases, this is a short-term concern related to change. We try to understand each individual's perceived productivity losses and work to address them. |
| There is more choice in workspace because of the variety of settings. | "Someone is sitting in my favorite spot. I just want to have my own place." | Workers can schedule and use a preferred seat when in the office, but spaces are only owned by workers with desk-based roles. |
| All spaces are available for anyone to use. | "I can't keep any personal items in the office." | Personalization is indeed difficult in a mobile work environment. We try to make up for this by working with local teams to decide how neighborhood groups can personalize their space. |
| There are more people at the same office (higher density), meaning that more people from the same department can work on the same floor. | "I have to fight for a place each time I come to the office." | We plan the number of seats to cover more than the typical office occupancy pattern. At times, when peak occupancy periods occur, drop-in and other spaces can be used to absorb the extra people. |
| Induction is faster; a new person overhears things at the office and learns faster. | "I overhear everything. It's disruptive—I can't concentrate." | The variety of spaces allows workers to choose an enclosed workspace when they need to concentrate. |

| A new team can be assembled quickly. | "Teams don't stay together for long because everyone's always on the go." | This is exactly the reason why we need to rethink the use of our office space—our employees are seldom desk-bound. |
|---|---|---|
| More meeting rooms and project rooms are available. | "All meeting rooms are being reserved by people wanting more privacy. I know, because I do it myself." | Some people do book these rooms for quiet work, but we monitor their use to assure fairness for all users. We reserve some spaces for last-minute group use. |
| There will be lower change costs, moving costs, and construction costs in the future. | "Why do we have to do this? What's in it for me?" | The autonomy to choose how and where to work to best suit each worker's needs—and the savings to the company in fixed costs—means that the company can invest in technology and training that directly affect a mobile worker's ability to succeed. |

Does FlexiSpace really cause employee productivity to drop like some skeptics fear? For an individual whose ego is closely tied to being in the corporate office, this may be the case. As with any change, workers go through a learning curve as they find ways to use the tools and support most effectively. At Nokia, we have not found any correlation between lower productivity and FlexiSpace—if it were there, it would be visible as lower results in performance reviews. We do know, however, that our real estate costs have come down and flexibility in the real estate portfolio has increased, positively affecting overall business performance.

Still, we acknowledge the fact that FlexiSpace is not for everyone. But with careful planning and consideration of workforce needs and work styles, organizations may find that it could work for them.

## Benefits of FlexiSpace

Organizations typically see the benefits of FlexiSpace very quickly, while individual employees often take longer to recognize the benefits. The organization, of course, realizes the following benefits:

- Less space dedicated to individual (under-occupied) desks allows more space for collaborative work or other value-adding spaces.

- Overall real estate cost savings can be invested in other performance-enhancing resources such as technology or training.

- More flexibility in space use allows organizations to accommodate variable headcounts over a period of time without having to add another desk every time a new person joins a team.

For individuals, the main benefit of FlexiSpace comes from expanding the variety of workplaces available to them:

- More autonomy and freedom to determine the place of work

- More collaborative spaces and higher availability of tools

- Better access to team members for effective collaborative work

- More flexibility to balance work and personal life

Mobile workers need and expect a combination of technology, workspace, and support systems that allows them to work in locations that suit their work processes and allow them to balance work and personal life. Supporting a mobile workforce must be an effort shared by various support functions (IT, real estate, human resources, security), because each has a role to play in making place perform for mobile workers.

Organizations planning to implement mobile work practices need to create and maintain support systems that allow mobile workers to be productive regardless of their location. Whether or not they choose to pursue telecommuting or FlexiSpace solutions, organizations should examine the way people work and then provide integrated solutions and support to make mobile work successful.

Simply adopting mobile work practices isn't enough for FlexiSpace to work—the technological infrastructure to support mobility has to be fully functional for FlexiSpace to gain acceptance.

# Things to Consider

- Management direction setting and involvement in planning are always crucial for a workplace change. Expand your horizons of what constitutes a workplace and how it can best be supported.

- Technology to support mobility is essential. This includes laptops, mobile devices, WLAN, and so on. Providing flexible workplace models without the supporting infrastructure is not likely to produce good results.

- Mobility increases the need for information security. What security policies and best practices does your organization need to implement to protect mobile workers and your corporate information?

- Working from home complements mobile workplace solutions in the office because it reinforces mobile work patterns. However, to be effective, this type of work needs to take the worker's job responsibilities into account.

- If your organization is going mobile, the way that offices are used will inevitably change. You can choose to proactively address that change or continue with your old way of allocating space. Flexible seating allocation produces quantifiable cost savings. Is it a good option for your organization?

- Change management for workplace projects is much easier if work becomes more mobile first and real estate changes are made later, when people realize how mobile they have already become.

- FlexiSpace requires day-to-day management—having clear desk policies, providing means to book meeting rooms, managing supplies, and so on. Agreeing on protocols for space use helps smooth the transition.

- Adjustable furniture is important for effectively supporting multiple users occupying the same workspace over time.

- Behavioral change takes time—the first two months or so often form a transition period during which local issues need to be addressed.

# 9

# Managing a Mobile Workforce

*In a world where our employees' knowledge is our greatest
asset, we see mobility as an essential element in Nokia's
HR strategy. Since innovation doesn't always happen "on
the clock" and our global teams can't always be together,
we are evolving to a way of working that transcends the
boundaries of time and place by taking full advantage
of converging technologies that connect employees
to their work. Along the way we have faced some
challenges—including changing management practices
and work behaviors—but the opportunities are significant.
Increasingly, our people have the freedom to work in ways
that best suit their work and personal life needs.*

—Hallstein Moerk, Global Head of Nokia Human Resources

Managing a mobile workforce is not something you start thinking
about after everyone has moved out of the corporate office and
the "for rent" sign is up. On the contrary, a key aspect of going
mobile involves managing a dynamic, on-the-go, and out-of-sight

workforce spread across multiple time zones. When Nokia began adding mobile capabilities to its business operations, concerns about managing the people aspect of a mobility transition began to surface:

- Managers expressed concerns that reduced face time created a situation that less scrupulous workers could exploit (a twist on the "while the cat's away, the mice will play" attitude).

- Line managers struggled to create a basis for measuring worker performance since they could not visibly confirm that workers were being productive with the time available to them.

- Employees complained that they missed the social dimension of work—face-to-face teamwork, informal communication in the office, and so on.

- Knowledge managers expressed alarm over potential security breaches to sensitive information as employees began working in public places using unsecured networks.

- Human resources (HR) people drew attention to the risk of burnout in employees who tended to overwork themselves because of inadequate self-management skills.

What are experiences like this teaching us? Above all, we have learned that before an organization can truly benefit from mobility, it has to prepare its workforce and overall corporate culture for mobility. People will find ways to use the tools and technologies for their personal benefit, but the organization can help clarify how these new work practices benefit overall team performance. Consequently, Nokia is working hard to decide how to adjust workforce management policies, practices, processes, and approaches to support a successful mobile organization.

# How Mobility Affects Workforce Management

As we have considered ways to manage Nokia's growing mobile workforce, we have begun to view the challenge as a set of three overlapping circles (Figure 21). Each circle represents a key dimension of workforce management and development: organization; policies and practices; and people, behaviors, and relationships. At the core of this evolutionary change are our managers, who themselves are affected by mobility but also act as change agents in implementing mobile work practices within their teams.

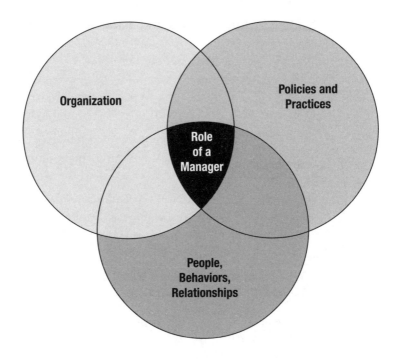

Figure 21. Areas of workforce management.

We realized that to develop a successful mobile organization, we had to identify which aspects of our operational and organizational model are affected by mobility, and then determine the best way to begin dealing with the changes. Although Nokia is still in the early stages of implementing its mobilization strategy, we present what we have learned so far about the effects of mobility on workforce management.

## Organization

Most businesses that begin shifting their workforce to more mobile ways of working will be faced with new but seemingly familiar management challenges. While traditional forms of management will continue for some time, mobility will add more layers of organizational complexity that business decision makers, managers, and HR need to consider in the earliest stages of mobility planning. Many of these challenges can be grouped under the following broad topics:

- Creating an environment that supports mobile work
- Shifting to a more global and external focus

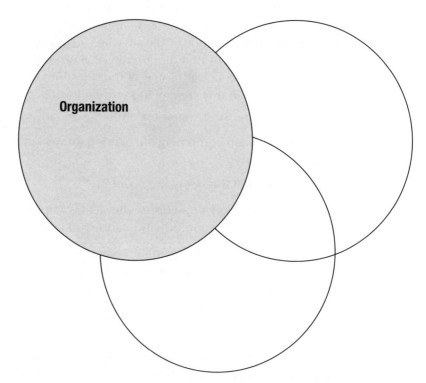

Figure 22. The organization.

### Creating an Environment that Supports Mobile Work

**Redefining the workday.** Creating a mobile workforce spread across time zones causes the traditional workday to lose its importance. Mobile workers will shape their working times to best meet their individual performance needs as well as the needs of their team. For example, a worker based in the United States who works from home may choose to be available in the early morning to cover Europe and the Americas, and again late at night to cover Asian time zones. However, the person might not take calls in the middle of the day in order to concentrate on individual work and have personal time. Organizations will need to create and cultivate an environment that supports this type of flexible approach to work and focuses on delivering results.

**Redefining the workplace.** Over time, the ability to work will depend less and less on location. Instead, working from any location with access to critical information will become the norm. Organizations should recognize and support the idea that their employees can work from practically anywhere. They will also need to identify work practices that require physical presence and plan for the associated travel costs. Some of the questions to ask when developing policies in this area include the following:

- Which roles are most suited for mobile work arrangements?

- What training and equipment are needed for working at home and/or remotely?

- Which costs will the company cover?

- Which policies and procedures should be implemented to ensure the security of information and workers?

At Nokia, we are seeing a gradual evolution of the corporate office into a social center rather than simply a place where people go to work. For example, some people come to the office when they have meetings but stay home when they have individual work to do. We are also seeing people setting up "chance" encounters— consciously choosing to sit in a public office area (such as a cafe) on some mornings and work wirelessly so that they can see and be seen by other people who work there—thus avoiding the need to schedule formal meetings. Face time really does have value, but it is leveraged more strategically in a mobile work mode.

**Redefining the value of work:** The demand for immediate access to information necessary for decision making is increasing every day. Mobilizing a workforce will make it easier for decision makers to contact knowledgeable workers—people who understand a topic because of their experience and studies—when they need to. Since instant access to the right information will make decision makers more accountable for their decisions, workers' knowledge and experience will become more

> Mobility is about using a set of mobile technologies and strategies to change business communication and collaboration patterns.

valuable than their location. The more a worker is recognized as an expert in a specific subject, the more decision makers will trust and consult that knowledge when they are faced with difficult decisions. This will prompt businesses to redefine the value of work based on the knowledge of workers and their contribution to important business activities.

### Shifting to a More Global and External Focus

**Virtual teams assembled from a global pool.** Because mobility promotes virtual teaming by providing access to qualified internal and external resources from different parts of the world, businesses will be able to quickly assemble best-in-class project teams regardless of geographic boundaries. While access to the best-qualified resources is an attractive benefit, managers will have to pay extra attention to other aspects of assembling a high-performing team, including rapidly integrating new team members who might be located across the globe and agreeing on processes and practices for information and knowledge management.

**Developing relationships with mobile knowledge workers.** Given that mobility allows virtual teams to form and dissolve as needed, organizations will need to develop the ability to quickly engage and disengage with mobile knowledge workers. Using track record and reputation as criteria for evaluating and selecting the right candidates is one potential approach. As organizations consider entering in these types of relationships, they should address the following topics with mobile knowledge workers before signing contracts with them:

- Are their mobile systems compatible with the organization's infrastructure, systems, and devices?

- Do they have certifications and/or experience in existing business processes, tools, and procedures?

- Do they already have internal clearance (non-disclosure agreement signed, corporate ID issued, intranet access granted, etc.)?

- Do they have established internal and external relationships (do they have a positive track record, are they known by decision-makers, are there any conflicts of interest, etc.)?

- Does their work style mesh with the organization's style?
- Have they shown their ability to work in a distributed team?
- Does their availability align with the organization's needs?
- Can they work with a team comprised of individuals with diverse personalities and opinions?

**External interaction.** As companies become more mobile in their work patterns, externally facing mobile workers and teams will need to agree on how they will work with their extended networks (e.g., partners and contractors). Expect that external partners will prefer different ways of working and work patterns. Planning for these and other teaming situations ahead of time will speed up the integration of new team members and maintain the workforce's efficiency.

## Policies and Practices

HR policies and practices should keep mobile employees motivated and engaged while providing line managers with support in developing high-performing mobile teams. This is easier said than done—to be effective, mobility needs to be considered in relation to all aspects of an organization's HR strategy. As we have examined opportunities to enhance the overall employee value proposition at Nokia, mobility has become a key factor. We believe that giving people more autonomy over their work increases commitment to the organization. In the same vein, having tools that enhance performance makes people feel more successful and hence more satisfied with their work. Along the way, we have challenged certain policies and practices in our effort to maintain a systemic view of the implications of mobility. In previous chapters, we have mentioned telecommuting, remote working, and security policies and guidelines; in this chapter, we outline other HR policies and practices that should be reviewed to better support mobile working.

Organizations considering the effects of mobility on their business should include the following HR policies and practices in their review:

- Transition management
- Diversity

- Training and development
- Employment policies, contracts, and benefit packages
- Performance measurement

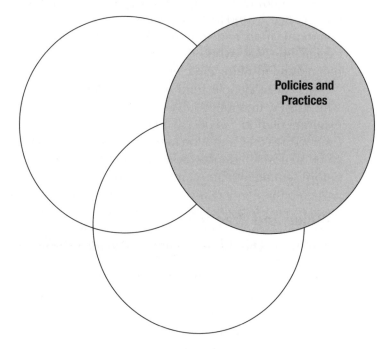

Figure 23. Policies and practices.

### Transition Management

The transition from traditional to mobile work practices is an evolutionary process and requires a change in mindset, attitude, and behaviors. Although Nokia is still in the early stages of implementing mobile working globally, we firmly believe that developing a change strategy early in the process and then implementing it are crucial for the success of the transition to mobile working.

**For those who go mobile.** While many workers may embrace more mobile ways of working, others may resist the change for several reasons: fear of the unknown, fear of not excelling in a mobile work environment, low technical aptitude, or because they simply do not agree with the direction. It is important to address these concerns and to build awareness and understanding through communication and training. A mobility transition plan should explain the way workers have been categorized and the logic behind any resulting policies.

Since most people tend to test the limits of the situations in which they find themselves, organizations should encourage experimentation—expect workers to see just what they can and cannot do as they transition to mobile roles. The organization and its workforce will undoubtedly move through a trial and error process before settling into an established work pattern. Smart businesses will keep this in mind as they develop transition plans; it will allow them to clearly articulate the boundaries of acceptable behavior and performance when working in a mobile way.

**For those who stay in a traditional work environment.** Although the focus will be on moving certain groups of employees into mobile roles, do not forget to plan how to explain the change for those who continue to work in a traditional environment. For example, some employees in more traditional roles will want to add mobility to their work routines. They are likely to challenge their managers on this issue, especially if some members of their team are already working in a mobile mode.

At Nokia, we discussed at length how to manage the transition for people who did not move into mobile roles. In the end, we decided that since many cases were unique, the most effective way to handle the situation was to define mobile work types, develop clear policies for what constituted a mobile worker, and then allow line managers to approve possible exceptions. We recommended that managers of mixed teams work with interested, traditional employees to identify how mobility could help them with their existing responsibilities. If concrete benefits existed, they were free to develop plans for working in a more mobile mode. Other approaches include training or transferring these individuals early in the transition. The main point here is that clear policies are vital for a smooth transition from traditional to mobile work practices.

## When Working Mobile Is Already the Norm

Throughout this book we have treated mobility as a relatively new concept that requires careful planning and implementation. While this is true in many cases, some roles have always been mobile. For example, sales and field forces are mobile by nature—their work takes them wherever the customer or cable box or telephone line happens to be. Because people in these roles are already familiar with mobile work modes, the kind of support they need during a transition to mobile work practices may vary considerably from the parts of the organization that are fundamentally changing their work and management practices. For example, naturally mobile workers will probably not suffer short-term productivity losses as their teams become virtual, because they have already developed methods for maintaining contact with virtual co-workers. They may only need training on new mobile devices and orientation to new, corporate-wide policies regarding mobile work. In fact, one of the benefits of evolving to mobile work practices is that it builds an infrastructure of mobility policies, guidelines, and practices that may have been lacking before.

### *Diversity*

After identifying which types of workers and functions are most suitable for mobile working, it is important to consider the cultural implications of mobility. While organizations may decide that a certain group of workers is ideal for mobile working, they may face cultural resistance to making the transition. For example, in some cultures face-to-face time in the office is an important and expected work practice. On the other hand, in some work settings, such as call centers, it is quite common for employees to work away from the office.

Mobile working can be a great way to support diversity initiatives. The key is to develop an understanding of and appreciation for different work practices, styles, and cultures across the organization. Including these factors as decision-making criteria will be crucial for a successful mobile work environment. Furthermore, it is important to think about and address the impact of mobility in the corporate diversity strategy and initiatives. For example, in defining diversity at Nokia, work location and geographic location are two of the twenty-four dimensions on its diversity wheel. Accounting for diversity in ways of working (where, when, how, and with whom) is a key factor in determining how Nokia operates on a daily basis in many areas.

### Training and Development

In a mobile environment, both businesses and employees emphasize and value flexibility, opportunities to gain experience, and increased options for learning and development. One way to help workers become more mobile in their work is to create personal development plans that provide opportunities to experience mobile work patterns. This approach considers how employees learn and develop on the job, and then blends these aspects into the learning activity with tools that develop the competencies necessary for the transition to mobile ways of working.

At Nokia, we are developing and adopting a wide range of learning tools that support mobile work patterns. For example, e-briefings, virtual classroom sessions, and mobile information nuggets all enhance the learning experience and support the concept of mobility in the workforce. Since many of Nokia's employees currently work on extended teams, and often in remote locations, virtual learning and mobility have become a necessity. In addition, many of our leadership development programs are designed to address fundamental concepts such as virtual teaming and networking in global teams. In essence, Nokia tries to emphasize the experiential components of learning by including mobile elements: the context of the learning activity becomes as important as the content.

### Employment Policies, Contracts, and Benefit Packages

While always important, unambiguous employment policies are critical to a successful mobility initiative. Businesses should develop and implement clearly worded policies that establish what is required for workers to transition to a mobile mode of working. Clearly outlining the policies and practices that employees will be required to comply with helps avoid misunderstandings. As Nokia has begun to move more of its workforce to mobile work modes, the guiding principle has been that any mobile work arrangement should not override the actual employment contract and benefits.

Over time, mobile work practices are likely to generate new types of contracts between businesses and individuals. When that happens, agreements, contracts, and benefit packages should 1) clearly define a reasonable division of time between work and personal life, 2) establish performance expectations, and 3) provide benefit coverage while workers are mobile—even across national boundaries. For example, with the ability to pull resources from a global pool, businesses will concentrate on building relationships with highly-skilled knowledge workers who can work anywhere and anytime. Potential service demands from other time zones may allow these knowledge workers to move away from traditional eight-hour workdays toward more flexible schedules.

This kind of relationship could be analogous to a retainer-based system, where a person agrees to reserve a specific amount of time to focus on a specific business need. To illustrate, many lawyers work on retainer. In this situation, time demands fluctuate: on some occasions, the time demand is heavy; in other situations, it is not. Compensation for an arrangement like this can be based on an hourly rate or on a fixed monthly sum regardless of how much of the reserved time is actually used. Work agreements for this type of relationship could be based on availability and resolution speed for specific problems. This would require a well-defined structure of expectations based on levels of urgency and capacity to accept and react to requests.

## Implementing a Home Office Policy

Organizations moving toward mobility should seriously consider creating a home office policy for their employees. This policy should cover the common aspects of working from home, including eligibility, definition of appropriate workspace, equipment and services provided by the organization, division of incurred costs, and security protocols. Also important is reviewing local labor laws and taxation issues, as well as the impact that working from home might have on insurance and other company-provided benefits. These vary by country, so local HR organizations need to be involved. Also, the local HR department usually has the best understanding of cultural issues that could affect working from home.

Workers must ensure that the workplace at home meets requirements for safety, security, and ergonomics. The necessary hardware and software should be in place, and, for security reasons, all upgrading and maintenance should be performed by the organization's IT department. Workers must also be familiar with the organization's working culture and able to perform agreed-on tasks while working from home (or from another remote location). Only job tasks that can be measured and independently carried out should be assigned to home office workers.

Managers should study the suitability of working from home for each worker. Of equal importance is the manager's own capability to adequately manage this type of work mode. Managers also need to ensure that workers accomplish their assigned tasks and that those tasks are measurable and clearly defined. Finally, managers should be supported by HR when their workers begin to work from home.

### Performance Measurement

As we have begun to shift to more mobilized work patterns at Nokia, we have discovered that managers need to work closely with their mobile employees to develop clearly defined performance measurements that are meaningful and relevant to actual work tasks. As dependence on task achievement grows, emphasizing high individual performance and positive contribution to the virtual team becomes more important.

Many managers accustomed to traditional methods of measuring performance will have to adjust their focus. Instead of looking at the energy spent on activities, the number of hours worked, and presence in a physical work location, managers should emphasize and measure their mobile workers' results and outputs. When a worker first enters a mobile position or starts a project, the manager and the worker should clearly define the tasks that the worker is expected to perform and the results she is to achieve. They should then explicitly define how the worker's performance will be measured. This activity establishes concrete parameters that both parties can turn to when productivity or performance questions arise. It also provides a basis for re-evaluating projects that have changed in scope since their original definition. An added benefit is that explicitly defined tasks provide the foundation for truly performance-based incentive programs.

Mobile workers should be able to exercise a significant amount of control over their performance goals and should be willing to accept full responsibility for achieving those goals. Managers should focus on creating performance measurements for mobile workers in the following key areas:

- Productivity and efficiency
- Change agility
- Renewal and innovation
- Cultural and team improvement

As always, it is important to establish a clear connection between the worker's performance goals and the organization's overall business strategy. The challenge is to develop new systems that accurately measure mobile workers' performance. This can be especially difficult for workers who have not worked in a mobile mode before (for example, a typical office worker who can now perform most of his tasks from a home office).

## People, Behaviors, and Relationships

How organizations choose to handle the area of people, behaviors, and relationships will in large part determine the success of their mobile workforce management efforts. At Nokia, we are discovering that the following areas are vital to our mobility efforts:

- Building trust between manager and worker
- Emphasizing personal responsibility and decision making
- Managing productivity expectations
- Balancing work and personal life
- Resolving worker concerns

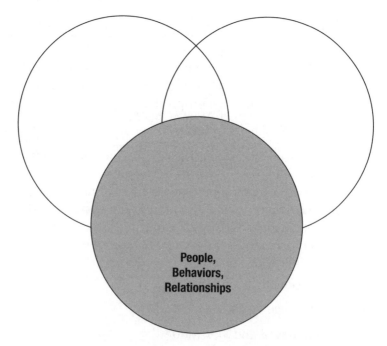

Figure 24. People, behaviors, and relationships.

### Building Trust Between Manager and Worker

Since a more mobile workforce means less face-to-face time between managers and employees, the need for a trusting relationship between managers and employees becomes paramount. The challenge is two-fold: 1) how to develop a sense of trust in a virtual situation and 2) how to help the manager ensure that employees are working appropriately (i.e., not too much and not too little). An added challenge is that the feeling of losing control over mobile employees can be stressful for managers and may result in resistance to mobility.

To overcome these challenges, both parties have to focus more on building a foundation for trust. Mobile workers need to build respect and trust in the eyes of their managers by demonstrating an ability and willingness to perform well. At the same time, managers need to let go and empower workers to take the initiative and make decisions. Agreeing on expectations and ways of working at the beginning of the working relationship is a good practice, and staying in touch through periodic check-ins is another good habit to develop.

It is also worth mentioning that, unless the recruitment process has already selected individuals who can adapt easily to a mobile work mode, managers may need to employ different techniques to build trust with different people. For instance, some employees may still want a higher level of supervision to feel comfortable working in a mobile mode. This is especially true with employees who are not convinced that their role should be mobile.

By engaging in behaviors that promote trust, managers will feel comfortable that their workers are being productive and responsive. At the same time, workers will feel that their managers trust them to get the job done because of minimal micromanagement and lack of excessive questioning.

### Emphasizing Personal Responsibility and Decision Making

Moving to an operational model that allows more mobility creates a risk for business owners and mobile workers. Because mobile workers are usually engaged in high-value/high-impact work tasks, the business is at risk if the mobile worker fails to perform or provide critical information when needed. As a result, mobile workers have great responsibility for completing their tasks, since they alone decide how, when, and where the task will be completed. To spread the risk, compensation and incentive packages could be tied more closely to performance—with an emphasis on availability, speed, and quality of problem resolution—as measured by its impact on the overall business. As always, the organization should strive to maintain an equitable balance between the work and personal life of each employee.

### Managing Productivity Expectations

When people can work almost anywhere and at almost any time, it is easy to develop the expectation that they will. This can lead to the following situations:

1. The ability to contact someone or access information at the moment of need creates a situation where workers will be expected to be available, provide information, or make decisions at a moment's notice—regardless of what they may be doing at the time.

2. As the average response time to requests decreases, people automatically start to expect increasingly shorter response times. This expectation can leave respondents feeling very stressed about providing a quick response. In addition, if the response is delayed even slightly, the requestor may feel irritated about the "long" response time.

3. Productivity expectations will increase as traditional downtime decreases since mobile workers can be productive while commuting, traveling, working off-site, and so on.

Businesses will have to carefully manage these and other expectations regarding when and how mobile employees work. For example, it should be perfectly acceptable for people to take breaks and be unavailable. At Nokia, some teams refer to this as optimizing sustainable productivity—an increased level of productivity that does not burn people out.

## *Balancing Work and Personal Life*

Increased expectations regarding availability, responsibility, and productivity will eventually erode the barrier between work and personal life. Organizations should be prepared to address this issue by doing the following:

- Develop management policies that ensure a minimum amount of intrusion into personal time (e.g., setting team protocols about when to expect others to be available).

- Address compensation issues that may arise as a result of excessive intrusion or overtime.

- Promote a culture that emphasizes and places high value on flexibility and quality of life.

> Mobility is about freedom of choice—it's not a forced directive to work 24/7 but an individual decision to work when and where it's most appropriate.

This topic is addressed in more detail later in this chapter (see section "Social and Cultural Aspects of Mobility").

## *Resolving Worker Concerns*

Some workers may express strong hesitation when asked to change the way they work—especially if they feel that the change is being imposed on them. While some of their concerns may be valid, much of this reaction is probably based on misperception and fear. Managers who acknowledge and directly address their workers' concerns will increase the level of trust and alleviate many of their worries.

To help organizations plan how to respond to their workers' concerns, we offer some of the most frequent reactions we have experienced at Nokia, as well as some suggested responses.

| Expressed concern | Underlying concern | Suggested response |
|---|---|---|
| "How will my boss and co-workers know when I've done something really good for the company?" | Worker fears missing recognition when no longer in the office and visible to co-workers. | Create regular company-wide and interdepartmental communication forums that share employee successes and concerns.<br><br>Set clear performance targets to help employees know that they will be rewarded for good performance. |
| "It's going to be too hard to find people and get a quick response if I'm not in the office." | Staying connected to colleagues requires more effort than working at the office. | Develop and deliver training on<br><br>managing and optimizing remote relationships<br><br>mobile technologies that help workers keep in touch<br><br>Ensure that workers take this training before they adopt a mobile role. |
| "Not enough thought has gone into this change." | Worker does not fully understand the benefits of mobile work and does not feel ready/capable to work in a mobile environment. | Identify and work through the reasons why the worker does not feel ready/equipped.<br><br>Carefully evaluate whether the worker, tasks, and team are truly suited for mobile work. |
| "This mobility thing means that I'm going to spend all of my time keeping people connected and none of my time making sure that any real work gets done." | Manager prefers to work with people in the office.<br><br>Manager prefers management by supervision.<br><br>Mobility puts too much responsibility on the manager to maintain connections between mobile workers. | Help managers understand that their role will change significantly.<br><br>Train managers on new mobile management strategies.<br><br>Evaluate whether the manager can adopt a new management style. |
| "How am I supposed to know if my team is working when I can't see them?" | Lack of face-to-face interaction lowers the level of trust between manager and workers.<br><br>Manager does not know how to ensure that her workers are being productive.<br><br>It is too difficult to identify clear objectives so performance reviews can be based on achievements. | Help the manager understand the importance of letting go and giving trust to build trust.<br><br>Suggest that the manager schedule periodic conference calls to check team's progress.<br><br>Support the manager in setting and evaluating objectives that measure achievement of tasks/results. |

| "The company is trying to save money by having me cover the costs of a home office." | Worker will incur personal expenses by working at home or while traveling. | Outline clear policies about what costs the company covers for home offices and travel. |
|---|---|---|
| | Work and personal time are going to overlap too much and it will be too hard to separate the costs that are specifically related to work and those related to personal needs. | Ensure that mobile workers are not required to bear costs that the company should cover. |
| | | Remind workers that not needing to come to the office results in personal savings: commuting costs (gas, wear and tear on vehicle, and time), wardrobe expenses, food costs, etc. |
| | | Help workers learn how to manage the balance between work and personal life. |

## Manager's Role in a Mobile Business

At Nokia, we are finding that some of the most dramatic changes caused by mobility involve the role of the manager. We now describe some of the key changes that our managers are going through to support their mobile workers and lead the transition to a mobilized business:

- Changing from supervisor to facilitator

- Hiring and retaining the best mobile performers

- Developing high-performing mobile teams

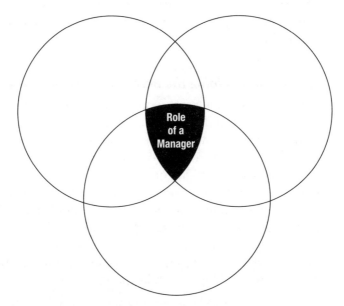

Figure 25. The manager's role.

### *Changing from Supervisor to Facilitator*

As our workforce becomes more mobile and global, we are discovering that traditional management practices and expectations like face time in the office and direct supervision are becoming less important. Our managers are finding themselves going through a paradigm shift, moving from a supervisory role to a facilitative role. Managers who successfully make this transition are able to do the following:

- Focus on coaching, supporting, and connecting team members and others.

- Orchestrate, integrate, and facilitate on a regular basis.

- Spend more time communicating with the team and between the team and other people.

- Spend more time and effort on planning and organizing.

- Concentrate on assigning the right talent or knowledge base to the right need and balancing the overall workload among team members.

Even after this transition, managers are still responsible for evaluating their workers' performance. To maintain acceptable performance levels, managers may need to look for new methods to motivate their mobile workers. Developing a strong, positive relationship with or a high level of influence over workers is a good way to encourage high performance. Another is to implement a real-time status reporting system that gives visibility into each worker's activities.

### *Hiring and Retaining the Best Mobile Performers*

As organizations begin to build mobile teams, they will need to focus on hiring and retaining the best mobile workers. Managers should identify existing workers who perform well in mobile roles and advocate their retention. When managers recruit candidates for mobile roles, certain competencies take on more importance. Soft skills like being flexible, dealing with ambiguity, influencing others, networking, making decisions, and taking the initiative may begin to outweigh competencies traditionally associated with the non-mobile form of those roles. From a management and leadership standpoint, in addition to having the previously mentioned soft skills, mobile managers must be competent in organizing and planning, integrating and synthesizing, building teams, and coaching.

Promoting the freedom of working mobile is a great way to attract and recruit new talent. However, job candidates should be comfortable with mobile work practices. As managers recruit new mobile workers, they should focus on the candidate's ability and willingness to adopt mobile work practices. For example, giving candidates a short overview of the team's mobile nature before making a final job offer provides a good foundation for setting expectations and ensures that candidates are aware of the work environment they will be entering. In addition, managers should have well-structured processes for quickly developing a productive mobile work relationship between a new employee and existing team members.

### Developing High-Performing Mobile Teams

**Creating the right working environment.** Managers should strive to optimize and adapt the work environment to get the highest productivity level out of their workers. Managers will need to focus their workers on high value-adding tasks, and ensure that all efforts quantifiably and positively affect the business. As high individual performance and contribution to the virtual team become more important, respect and trust between virtually connected team members will be based more on the ability to perform than on personality and interaction skills. Having said this, managers should still be prepared to handle conflicts between individuals with divergent styles. For example, some workers may prefer to work exclusively at home while others may come to the office for short periods to use the printers and high network bandwidth (or just to spend time in the office).

**Managing team dynamics.** Adopting a mobile way of working will change the dynamics of existing teams. For example, quick hallway discussions and ad-hoc meetings by the water cooler or coffee machine will diminish. Losing the sense of team membership and the social connectedness provided by a physical office can throw a wrench in the works of a traditional high-performance team. Managers of existing teams should expect to go through the forming-storming-norming-performing cycle again when the team transitions mobile work patterns. One way to ease the transition to mobile working is to encourage the open sharing of expectations and perceptions among team members.

**Establishing work patterns.** Maintaining high team performance in a mobile environment requires the manager and team members to work together to define, establish, and refine the team's work patterns. This includes agreeing on seemingly simple processes like decision making and communication. For example, how do members alert the distributed team that a key decision has been made? More importantly, how do managers ensure that the input of all team members is adequately included in the team's decision making? Also, because teams will be more globally distributed, part of developing a well-synchronized team includes considering the cultural background and perspective of each team member.

Another challenge in this area is agreeing on how the team is going to share information and knowledge. Finding and implementing the best tools, processes, and practices for sharing and managing information and knowledge is an important part of ensuring a mobile team's success. At Nokia, we are finding that establishing a virtual team room as the central hub of information is a helpful first step.

**Facilitating effective communication.** Because instant face-to-face interaction becomes difficult when working mobile, constant communication and the use of multiple media are crucial. Traditional communication methods like all-hands meetings are still effective but can be expensive for a globally distributed team. When used, such meetings should be carefully planned to maximize their value. Our experience with global, virtual teams has shown that periodic (usually quarterly) face-to-face meetings supplemented with conference calls and written statements are important to get teams off to a good start (particularly new teams). Once a virtual team passes the initial stages of formation, staying connected on a regular basis via conference calls and online meetings becomes much easier. In addition, seeking out informal means to "see" one another even while mobile can be very helpful; for example, instant messaging buddy lists and presence indicators can help team members know when their colleagues are available for an informal chat.

In a remote work environment, having access to mobile technologies makes it easier for workers to quickly contact other team members. As long as they are not in a cold spot (a place with no connectivity), they can usually contact another team member via text messaging, telephone, instant messaging, email, or some other method. For example, the mobile infrastructure that we are developing at Nokia lets our internal teams make secure conference calls while in non-traditional work settings by using their mobile devices.

# Social Aspects of Mobility

We recognize that finding the ideal solution for managing the social aspects of mobility will always be a work in progress. What Nokia has decided to do may not be exactly suitable for other companies. However, we share the following ideas here in the hope that other companies will be able to learn from our experience and apply it to their own situation.

As Nokia has moved more of its workforce out of the office, the risks associated with isolated team members and communication breakdowns have begun to surface. For example, while team members have been able to maintain a good level of individual productivity, in some cases team interaction has dropped. Even though new communication tools and technology have been available, most workers have ignored them and chosen their own comfort zone for work. Even for teams with members who have worked together well in the past, losing face-to-face interaction has slowed the process of building team unity and communication.

> If you're serious about mobilizing your business, start looking now for ways to remotely create the social interaction that occurs naturally in a corporate office.

As a result, project managers and team leaders have had to spend more time understanding and managing this problem. The obvious remedy—bring everyone together more often—has not been a good solution because the cost of bringing a mobile team together physically on a regular basis easily becomes prohibitive. The mobile work environment has caused more sociable team members to look for new ways of interaction.

We are finding that as organizations adopt a more mobile operating mode, they need to set new expectations for work behaviors. It is also important to create forums that cultivate corporate culture and enable social interaction that occurs naturally in a physical office. Nokia is addressing this situation methodically by carrying out the following measures:

- Acknowledge that mobile working is different from what we have known in the past and discuss this openly with workers.

- Provide easy-to-use tools that integrate naturally into employee work routines.

- Encourage a continuous change in behavior and interaction habits through direct and indirect means.

We have started by implementing online collaboration systems that provide audio and video feeds as well as instant messaging and chat forums. To encourage changes in work behavior, we have begun to arrange training sessions, plan informational meetings, and distribute publications with the latest information on tools, tips, and tricks. We are also initiating an effort to circulate worker success stories to help people feel more involved in the activities of their co-workers.

## Keeping Work Social

To keep work social, start planning and preparing early for the changes that will occur in social interaction as the workforce adopts a more mobile work mode. The following list contains some social aspects of work to consider.

### Virtual water cooler/coffee machine

In the physical office, all of the interesting stuff happens at the water cooler or around the coffee machine. A large amount of small talk, gossip, and personal interaction takes place there. Going mobile does not reduce the need for social interaction—on the contrary. Informal social interaction is critical to building strong working relationships. For mobility initiatives to be successful, organizations need to provide alternative channels for informal social interaction between mobile, remote, and office workers—in other words, virtual water coolers and coffee machines.

### Balance between work and personal life

Mobility thins and, at times, blurs the line between working time and time off. If businesses do not establish and maintain a balance between work and personal life, their workers will—possibly in ways that are not mutually beneficial. For example, workers may begin to gravitate toward cold spots as an excuse for not being available. Establish the balance with workers before allowing more mobility in their routines. This ensures that workers remains productive and demonstrates that the organization cares about its workers.

### Cultural and regional differences

Establishing mobile work practices based on specific technologies may not always work well across cultures. For example, some cultures place high value on silence and clarity of thought with minimal verbal interaction. Other cultures value a high degree of verbal exchange to ensure the alignment of thoughts and understanding between individuals. The first culture would most likely adopt a text-based communication system, while the second would embrace a voice-based system.

Some cultures are more accepting and tolerant of technology in their lifestyle than others. These cultures adopt technology as a way of life and have a strongly consumption-driven population that demands and embraces the advancement, integration, and frequent change of technology. Integrating mobility into this lifestyle would be perceived as progress and a natural development. Other cultures, in contrast, value direct interaction and prefer to minimize the use of technology: voice might be the only mobile technology that they regularly use. In these cultures, technological advancements are primarily driven by business needs rather than consumer demand. Members of these cultures do not consider technology an essential part of their lifestyle. Organizations with substantial employee populations from both cultures will have to carefully consider how their mobility initiatives will account for each culture's needs and preferences.

### Privacy must be ensured before adoption increases

The growing ability to track and locate an individual via their mobile device creates serious concerns for privacy advocates. There are also concerns related to unscrupulous mobile service providers that could possibly monitor and intercept confidential information as mobile workers conduct business within their service domain. Restricting unauthorized access to personal information while an individual is mobile and working across multiple domains is the first step to building trust and increasing user adoption. Resolving these issues has become a top priority for Nokia. Fortunately, good solutions are available today for establishing secure connections to corporate information systems.

### Neo-Renaissance of individualism

As we look forward, mobility could potentially move businesses from organizationally driven societal architectures (i.e., communities and social activities within larger companies) to societal architectures centered on the individual. Communities of knowledge and virtual greenhouses of specialized knowledge would begin to emerge. For example, instead of hiring a person to work as an in-house expert in a specific technology, a business could sign a contract with a special interest community for access to expert knowledge on an as-needed basis. One look at the personal networks of today's young people gives a good indication of the relative unimportance of proximity in establishing and maintaining knowledge networks in the future. Agreements between businesses and these communities may become the building blocks of a virtual workforce that provides knowledge on demand through access to a knowledgebase or personal consultation. Business owners should begin studying which areas of knowledge expertise are mission-critical to the business, and which areas could be accessed virtually if needed.

### Guard against too much isolation and independence

Remember, mobile work is *not* synonymous with independent work. Many people can and do use the workplace as a hub for interaction, social networking, and getting a sense of the buzz of the organization. (If some mobile workers seem to have forgotten this, they may need a gentle reminder to come to their corporate office occasionally to maintain that connection.) Clearly, interaction is critical to most of today's business practices, but so is the feeling of belonging to a community. Too often we equate mobile work with lonely work. But many mobile workers find places where they can be among people even though they are not in the office—just look at all the people working in coffee shops and airline clubs.

# Things to Consider

Transitioning from traditional to mobile work practices is an evolutionary and sometimes difficult process—it requires a change in mindset, attitude, and behavior from both managers and workers.

- How adaptable is your workforce? Have they shown the ability to adapt quickly to changing business conditions?

- Not all workers know how to work while on the go—successfully mobilizing a workforce requires clear management policies and practices together with proper training to develop appropriate work habits and maintain productivity while mobile.

- How much effort will be required to add mobility requirements and task-based performance measurements to your existing people management practices and policies?

You can reduce change resistance by helping your workforce understand their value and contribution to your changing organization.

- How will you ensure a smooth transition from traditional to mobile ways of working in your current workforce? How will this affect your corporate culture and interaction between managers and workers?

- Managing a mobile workforce requires a high level of trust between manager and worker. What strategies can your organization implement to help managers empower their employees to make important decisions and encourage them to take greater responsibility for their performance while mobile?

Establishing and maintaining social relationships is difficult as workers become more mobile and separated—a higher level of communication and collaboration is needed to ensure a high level of team performance and adequate social interaction.

- What systems and practices will your business need to implement to ensure quick and effective communication and collaboration within a mobile virtual team?

- How would you go about creating virtual water coolers and coffee machines?

# Work Goes Mobile

# 10

# Building Business Cases for Mobility

*At first we struggled with the business case for mobility. Then we
realized that, like email, mobility is just part of doing business.
This "ah-ha" moment freed us to move forward with a few
mobility solutions. The results were astounding—for example,
real-time access to email and calendar makes my life incredibly
flexible. It's a huge advantage at this level of business.*

—*John Robinson, Senior VP of Services, Operations, and Quality*
*Nokia Enterprise Solutions*

Building a business case is rarely a simple task, even if the process
itself is relatively well known. When the mobility team reached the
point of building business cases for the potential mobility solutions
they had identified, they faced the challenge of developing solid
cases for a new, evolving area of business infrastructure where many
benefits are qualitative and not always immediately apparent.

In the process of building their cases, the team learned that a good mobility business case 1) contains carefully considered assumptions, 2) presents realistic scenarios, and 3) includes a detailed analysis of potential benefits. We have mined the team's experience and combined our findings with common business case development practices to present a sound method for developing mobility cases. As a result, this chapter presents the following:

- A description of some of the unique characteristics of mobility solutions and suggestions on how to deal with them in a business case

- A method for building mobility business cases

- An illustration of the method using the Nokia Networks repair and return process as an example (see Chapter 6)

- A method for comparing mobility business cases

# Unique Characteristics of Mobility Solutions

Most organizations happily invest in laptops, email infrastructure, and PIM solutions because they have been around for a while. They have evolved into standardized, well-defined, neatly packaged offerings with clearly understood costs and benefits. Consequently, they are often deeply embedded in the business infrastructure and are simply classified as part of the cost of doing business. But emerging mobile capabilities have yet to make their way into conventional corporate wisdom—they still have to overcome the inherent skepticism that follows any innovation.

Given this situation, solutions that add mobile elements to existing business activities have several unique characteristics that set them apart from other large-scale business solutions. The following table presents these characteristics along with suggested methods for addressing them in business cases.

| Characteristic | Successful business case |
|---|---|
| Mobility benefits typically have a strong workforce productivity component, which is difficult to quantify. | Include typical scenarios with arguments that support expected benefits. Basing these arguments on corporate business measures and providing projected savings in time, costs, and so on will improve the scenario's validity. |
| Mobile capabilities enable fundamentally new ways to design business processes. However, many business process owners do not clearly understand the ramifications of redesigning their processes with mobile elements. | Clearly explain the differences between the old process and the new process, and stress the impact on process and organizational structures. |
| Business decision makers are often skeptical about purported benefits of technologies that are not widely implemented and accepted, and are often less inclined to fund proposals based on such technologies. | Be realistic about the benefits of the proposed solution, and focus on well-defined deployment phases, each of which generates a tangible set of benefits (instead of waiting until the end of a "big bang" deployment to realize the benefits). |
| Because some mobility elements can be applied to multiple process areas, the complexity of defining the business case increases. | Focus on critical areas of the process which mobility can affect positively, whether those areas are limited to one process or apply to many. |
| In a large company, sharing benefits across organizational and/or administrative boundaries creates extra challenges. For instance, why should group A invest in and implement a mobility solution when the benefits are also available to group B without the same investment? | Provide information for business owners and shareholders about the cross-organizational and cross-process impact of mobility. Including proposals for critical areas like benefit sharing and investment burden will facilitate the acceptance of the business case. |

# A Method for Developing Mobility Business Cases

The method we present here combines Nokia's own experience with a generally accepted approach to developing business cases. The following table describes each step in the method.

| Step | Fundamental question | Objective | Required materials | Expected outputs |
|------|----------------------|-----------|--------------------|------------------|
| 1. Validate future state. | What primary opportunities for improvement does the mobility solution offer? | Validate the proposed future state and document its key characteristics from a mobility perspective. | Current process maps<br>Solution outline | Future process maps<br>Clear documentation of improvement areas |
| 2. Identify key benefits. | What are the solution's key benefits, and what are their logical categories? | Discover the key benefits related to the improvements identified in the previous step. | Future process maps<br>Documentation of improvement areas | List of key benefits with definitions, measurement mechanisms, and targeted improvements |
| 3. Develop cost estimates. | What is the cost of developing and deploying the solution in the organization? | Develop estimates of the cost to develop and deploy the mobility solution. | Validated, high-level solution architecture | Estimated costs for hardware, software, and services |
| 4. Create and validate baseline business case. | What is the business case and how does it hold up against best/worst case scenarios? | Create a baseline business case for the mobility solution. | Validated solution architecture<br>Targeted benefits<br>Cost estimates | Documented business case |

Before applying this method, be sure to obtain the following information and materials:

- Documentation and other information about 1) the proposed solution and 2) its people, process, and technology requirements

- Personal knowledge of the business processes included in the solution or, at a minimum, access to subject matter experts

- Key performance indicators (KPIs), their definitions, methods used to collect data for them, and current and targeted values for each business process

- A detailed understanding of the user groups affected by the solution

- Access to standard corporate business case framework and associated tools

# Building a Business Case for a Mobility Solution

To illustrate how to build a mobility business case using this method, we examine the Nokia Networks repair and return process described in Chapter 6. Nokia Networks is a field service organization that performs maintenance on telecommunication and cellular equipment for Nokia's service customers. The CARE Hardware Services team performs the process of repairing and returning faulty hardware covered by customer service contracts.

## *Gathering Prerequisite Information*

As discussed in Chapter 6, evaluating the existing repair and return process from a mobility perspective resulted in several potential improvements. The information presented in Chapter 6 provides documentation on the proposed solution, as well as sufficient knowledge of the business processes and user groups involved. The following table lists KPIs typically associated with field service processes.

| KPI | Definition | Collection method | Current value | Targeted value |
|---|---|---|---|---|
| Open work orders per day | Total unresolved work orders in the system at the beginning of a workday | Work order system | 100 | 70 |
| Completed work orders per engineer per day | Number of work orders closed by an engineer in a day | Work order system | 10 | 13 |
| Average windshield time per engineer per day | Time spent driving between customer sites and office or warehouse | Timesheets and time reporting in work order system | 4 hours | 3 hours |
| Invoicing cycle time (for service) | Time between service completion and sending invoice | Combined information from work order, CRM, and billing systems | 10 days | 4 days |

### Validating Future State

The next step is to validate the proposed future state of the solution. Pay particular attention to new process information flows and to the user profiles that the solution addresses. It is important to validate the solution with key stakeholders—in this case, the people with operational responsibility for the CARE team and process. The questions listed below illustrate how to 1) validate the future state of the repair and return process and 2) obtain valuable insight into defining the business case.

#### Information flow

- How does information flow between the field engineer and the relevant Nokia corporate systems (trouble ticketing, work assignment, SAP, etc.)?

- How much of the field service process can be accomplished without real-time access to back-end systems?

- When does the engineer need real-time connectivity? For example, to comply with the SLA, relevant information could be dispatched to the field engineer together with the work assignment.

- How often does the field engineer need to synchronize the mobile device with back-end systems to maintain the integrity of the data and the process? Does the field engineer need real-time or right-time information? For example, repair vendor addresses could be treated as static reference information that changes infrequently while spare part availability would need to be updated at least daily.

- What are the time requirements for synchronizing information with the mobile device? For example, is once every 24 hours sufficient?

- Does the new information flow result in new capabilities? Two possible solutions are 1) making information accessible that was not previously available and 2) reducing the delay in updating back-office systems with information captured in the field.

#### Use Cases and User Profiles

- How will the mobilized process typically be used?

- Do all field engineers perform the same functions and have the same needs, or are they made up of distinct groups and profiles? Can they be characterized by how often they use the process, how critical their access is to the process, how they use the process, etc.?

- Do the user profiles dictate different device and peripheral requirements?
  - Non-rugged versus rugged: An executive might require a simple mobile device, but a field engineer could require a different device that can hold up to hard use.
  - Peripherals: A field engineer might need a camera, printer, SD or MMC card, barcode reader, and so on to perform her work, while an administrator might not have the same requirements.

**Input Mechanism**
- Will the field engineer enter data using a keyboard, a touch screen, or handwriting recognition software?

In this example, the validated future state of the repair and return process would be as follows:

- The field service engineer is equipped with a mobile device, a barcode scanner, and a portable printer.
- Work assignments (including customer address, maps, part numbers, etc.) are received and reports are sent using the mobile device. This requires integration with the trouble ticketing application.
- The equipment is used to electronically perform the following tasks:
  - Capture part numbers.
  - Identify the appropriate repair vendor and shipping address.
  - Print the shipping address and the Air Way Bill number on a sticker.
  - Locate the LSP's nearest pickup location.
- When the work assignment is completed, the engineer updates the details on the mobile device, triggering multiple messages to internal and external systems, including Nokia's SAP system, the LSP's systems, and the work order system.
- The engineer drops the faulty part at the nearest LSP pickup facility.
- The LSP sends the part to the correct repair vendor.

This validation process can also help identify needs not covered by the original solution. For example, there will be times when the field engineer needs real-time information but is outside of network coverage. A successful solution would assume that the engineer will not always be connected and would provide a disconnected alternative. In this case, the disconnected alternative could be a database stored on the mobile device. This database could be periodically synchronized with the master database—either when the engineer is within network coverage or at the Nokia office.

Understanding the future state of the repair and return process helps define how the solution improves the process, as highlighted in the table below. The first column presents a key feature of the solution, and the remaining columns present areas that the solution may improve. A checkmark shows that the solution will have a positive impact on the area.

| Key Solution Feature | Data accuracy | Reduction in repair cycle time | Reduction in problem resolution cycle time | Improved inventory management | Enhanced management of field service resources | Reduction in duplicate or manual work |
|---|---|---|---|---|---|---|
| Receive work assignments on mobile device | ✓ | | ✓ | | ✓ | ✓ |
| Assignment reporting and tracking with mobile device | ✓ | ✓ | ✓ | | ✓ | ✓ |
| Barcode scanning of part numbers | ✓ | | ✓ | ✓ | | ✓ |
| Repair vendor information on mobile device | ✓ | ✓ | | ✓ | | ✓ |
| Integration of LSP pickup and address information | ✓ | ✓ | | ✓ | | ✓ |
| Reporting material usage to back-office | ✓ | | | ✓ | | ✓ |

### Identifying Key Benefits

After validating the future state of the solution and identifying the areas of improvement, the next step is to identify the key benefits offered by the solution. This information sets the stage for creating the baseline business case. This step can be difficult because most mobility solutions to date have only focused on a few key business processes—the proposed solution may have a much wider scope.

The framework shown in Figure 26 builds on the four scorecard dimensions used at Nokia for evaluating business cases. It is useful for identifying and organizing the benefits of a mobility solution. Because most business managers understand the concept of a scorecard, using this framework also makes discussions about mobility solutions easier. In addition, the framework can be used as a tool to ensure that the proposed initiatives are valid and worth pursuing.

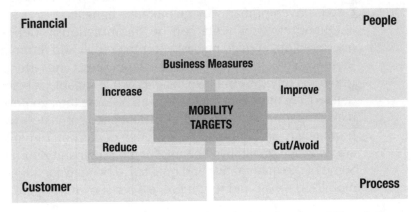

Figure 26. Four dimensions for identifying the benefits of a mobility solution.

The framework should be based on business measures that are set and tracked across the entire company. After identifying the solution's mobility targets and effects, the corporate measures can be used to assess the effect of the proposed mobility solution. Figure 27 presents some mobility targets that could apply to the mobilized repair and return process.

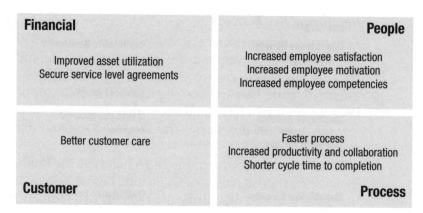

Figure 27. Potential mobility targets for the repair and return process.

The mobility targets can be used to define the expected benefits of the proposed mobility solution. In the context of developing and presenting business cases, it is especially important to distinguish between quantitative and qualitative benefits, and ensure that the case is driven primarily by quantitative benefits.

Quantitative benefits can be unambiguously defined and measured on an ongoing basis—for the repair and return process, these would be reduced material shipping costs and faster problem resolution times. Qualitative benefits, while capable of being tightly defined, are more difficult to measure because their contribution to real company performance is more difficult to correlate—workforce productivity and improved knowledge of customer installed base are two such qualitative benefits for the repair and return process. Some of the quantitative and qualitative benefits identified for the mobilized repair and return process are shown in Figure 28.

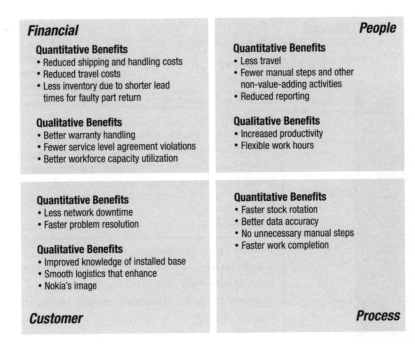

**Financial**

**Quantitative Benefits**
- Reduced shipping and handling costs
- Reduced travel costs
- Less inventory due to shorter lead times for faulty part return

**Qualitative Benefits**
- Better warranty handling
- Fewer service level agreement violations
- Better workforce capacity utilization

**People**

**Quantitative Benefits**
- Less travel
- Fewer manual steps and other non-value-adding activities
- Reduced reporting

**Qualitative Benefits**
- Increased productivity
- Flexible work hours

**Quantitative Benefits**
- Less network downtime
- Faster problem resolution

**Qualitative Benefits**
- Improved knowledge of installed base
- Smooth logistics that enhance
- Nokia's image

**Quantitative Benefits**
- Faster stock rotation
- Better data accuracy
- No unnecessary manual steps
- Faster work completion

**Customer**

**Process**

Figure 28. Mobility benefits for the repair and return process.

Distinguishing between quantitative and qualitative benefits and focusing on the quantitative ones makes the business case more compelling and improves the odds of it being approved and funded.

### Developing Cost Estimates

The next step is developing cost estimates. Two types of estimates need to be made:

- One-time, or capital expenditures (CAPEX): These costs include the acquisition and deployment of all components of the solution.

- Ongoing, or operating expenditures (OPEX): These are costs that the organization incurs to keep the solution operational and in line with business requirements.

After identifying one-time and ongoing costs, this step becomes an exercise in estimating the cost of the solution as accurately as possible.

As with other mobility solutions, the mobilized repair and return process included typical costs such as those listed in the following table.

| One-time costs | Hardware | Mobile devices, including peripherals<br>Server infrastructure<br>&bull; Application development and testing<br>&bull; Production environment<br>&bull; Device provisioning and management software<br>Network infrastructure, including investments in additional security and connectivity infrastructure to support the solution (firewalls, VPN concentrators, etc.)<br>Device activation |
|---|---|---|
| | Software | Device/client operating system<br>On-device software<br>&bull; Device management client<br>&bull; Security (connectivity, data encryption, personal firewall, antivirus, etc.)<br>Synchronization client<br>Middleware |
| | Services | Program/project management<br>Consulting (design, development, migration, and integration)<br>Internal full-time equivalent requirements<br>Training (users, developers, and IT admin, and support) |
| Ongoing costs | Maintenance | Licensing and support for relevant hardware and software (including devices) |
| | IT Support | IT help desk and support<br>Ongoing troubleshooting and enhancements |
| | Carrier | Network and airtime charges |
| | Training | Ongoing training for people using the new solution (e.g., training for new field engineers) |

### Creating and Validating a Baseline Business Case

The previously described steps provide the information needed to assemble a thorough business case for a mobility solution. The next step—creating a baseline business case—includes defining key inputs. In the case of the repair and return process, the key inputs include the following:

- Number of field service engineers

- Number of cases per year

- Estimated percentage of cases that could be managed using the new mobilized business process

- Percentage of faulty parts with an unknown status (no information on those parts in any application)

- Number of manual data entry steps that can be eliminated

- Percentage reduction in paper-based field reports (completed by engineers for each site visit)

- Reduction in incorrect shipping of faulty parts

- Average value of parts

- Process cycle time

- Time spent by material in transit

- Price of repair using a recycled part versus a new part

With these key inputs and the outputs from the previous steps, a baseline business case for adding mobile components to the repair and return process would project significant first-year savings. The table below shows how the outputs from each step in the method for business case development contributes to the baseline business case. The key benefit areas at the bottom of the table show the *monthly* savings across several areas as well as a *one-time* reduction in inventory in the repair cycle. Together the benefits result in a one-time annual savings of approximately five million euros. (Note that the figures are for illustrative purposes only.)

| Current process | |
|---|---:|
| Number of field service engineers | 1,000 |
| Number of cases handled per year | 175,000 |
| Cost of each manual data entry step | € 3.00 |
| Percent of faulty parts with unknown status | 10% |
| Handling cost per item with unknown status | € 80.00 |
| Average value of each part | € 200.00 |
| Cost of completing each fault report | € 0.35 |
| **Future mobilized process** | |
| Percent of cases managed by new mobilized process | 60% |
| Reduction in instances of incorrect shipping per case | 1 |
| Reduction in shipping costs per case | € 26.00 |
| Number of manual data entry steps eliminated | 2 |
| Average days saved in cycle time per case | 15 days |
| Percentage reduction in paper-based fault reports | 50% |
| **Costs** | |
| One-time solution rollout and training cost per user | € 200.00 |
| Service cost per user per month | € 75.00 |
| Peripherals (printer and scanner) cost per user per month | € 50.00 |
| **Intermediate calculations** | |
| Number of cases handled per year with mobile device | 105,000 |
| Number of cases handled per day with mobile device | 288 |
| Number of parts with unknown status per month | 875 |
| Number of paper-based fault reports per month | 4,375 |
| **Key benefit areas** | |
| Value of reduced inventory in repair cycle (one-time reduction) | € 863,014.00 |
| Reduction in costs due to reduced paper-based fault reports per month | € 1,531.00 |
| Savings on shipping costs per month | € 224,384.00 |
| Reduction in costs from eliminating duplicate data entry per month | € 51,781.00 |
| Savings on handling of unknown faulty items per month | € 70,000.00 |
| **Projected first-year savings** | € 5,018,525.00 |

When developing mobility business cases, do not underestimate the importance of two other factors in gaining approval and funding for the proposed solution:

- Solution positioning and communication. For example, a mobile solution for sales force automation might not be received well if it is positioned primarily as a method for each salesperson to provide accurate data to their managers. However, positioning it in the context of improving each salesperson's productivity and enhancing his or her ability to meet or exceed sales quotas increases the odds of success considerably.

- Process integration. Forcing workers to make drastic changes in their work habits is a guaranteed way to stop a mobility solution in its tracks—even if it does get funded. A successful mobility solution embeds itself within existing work routines, thus minimizing the need for adjustment.

The method we have presented here is just one of many good ways to develop business cases. Different organizations prefer different analysis approaches—Total Cost of Ownership (TCO), Net Present Value (NPV), or payback period, for instance. The results obtained from this method, however, can be translated into many of these other approaches.

# Comparing Mobility Solutions

The method we outlined for developing a mobility business case should result in an accurate initial definition of the benefits and costs of adding mobile elements to business activities. However, a business case by itself only measures the merits of a specific initiative in relatively isolated terms. It does not adequately account for the typical scenario in most organizations where several projects compete for limited investment resources during a planning and budgeting cycle.

Mobility solutions typically compete head-to-head with other investment projects. Comparing mobility solutions is useful for ensuring that only the most compelling cases compete with non-mobility projects. When comparing mobility solutions, the business case becomes just one dimension in the process of deciding which solution should compete for approval and funding.

The following qualitative framework is useful for quickly identifying the relative merits of several mobility projects.[1] This approach assesses mobility solutions across the following four dimensions (Figure 29):

- Technology invasiveness

- Expected benefits

- Solution reach

- Degree of process/people change

[1]This framework is not intended to replace the sophisticated, formal portfolio management techniques presented in business management literature. Rather, it provides a way to quickly compare several mobility solutions.

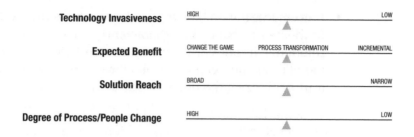

Figure 29. Framework for comparing mobility solutions.

Evaluating mobility solutions through these dimensions makes it easy to compare them and determine which one would have the best chance of competing with other, non-mobility projects for funding. Each of the four dimensions is described below.

**Technology Invasiveness**
If the mobility solution uses technology, it will interact with the existing technology infrastructure. If a business process relies heavily on technology, the effort to mobilize the process will probably require modifying the technology infrastructure. The more a process depends on technology (for example, modifying customer data in the CRM system), the more complex the effort to add mobile elements becomes (and the more likely it will be to disrupt a core business system). This dimension ranges from high to low invasiveness and is measured by evaluating the following factors:

- Integration of corporate back-ends and associated adapters or connectors

- Number of disparate back-ends affected by mobilization

- Organization of data prior to dispatch and delivery to the end user

**Expected Benefits**
Part of developing a business case for a mobility solution includes identifying and understanding the expected benefits to the organization. Depending on the nature of the solution, the potential benefits could belong to one of the following categories:

- **Incremental.** This category includes the most elementary productivity and efficiency benefits. Typically achieved by replacing paperwork with automated processing, these benefits are all about improving the operational efficiency of a process. Mobility projects that focus on intelligent use of workers' time by untethering them and providing access to information when needed—or by sending relevant information to them in an asynchronous fashion—typically provide benefits of this type. Incremental benefits, while seemingly simple, can be quite attractive.

  > When benefits cross business unit or administrative boundaries, you need to be clear on how to split those benefits.

- **Process Transformation.** When mobility changes a business process, it can achieve results that address any of the three value disciplines—operational excellence, product leadership, and customer intimacy. For example, a retailer deploys a mobile solution in its warehousing department. The new process increases visibility into the retailer's supply chain. This has major implications for the retailer, which can streamline its supply chain operations and thereby achieve a degree of competitive differentiation. At the same time, the supply chain becomes more responsive.

- **Change the Game.** Using mobility as a tool can transform an entire organization and, potentially, its ecosystem as well. It can launch a new business or even result in a new business model for the industry.

The distinction between these three categories is of course not definitive—a benefit might fall into more than one category. Although most organizations would like to see straightforward mobility projects that provide change-the-game types of benefits, that is usually not the case. The projects that provide the most far-reaching benefits are often the most complex. To balance risk versus reward, smart business managers invest in a good mix of the easy (incremental), moderate (process transformation), and complex (change the game) projects. Most real-world projects provide incremental benefits; some can transform processes; and a few change the game.

### Solution Reach

Solution reach describes how many workers will be affected by the proposed mobility solution. A solution that mobilizes a horizontal process used by most employees in the organization will affect far more employees than a vertical solution that only mobilizes a small percentage of the workforce.

### Degree of Process/People Change

When a business process goes mobile, technology is usually a small part of the overall solution—process and people issues occupy a large percentage of the solution. By definition, mobilizing a business process implies modifying to some extent the way that people perform the process. The degree of change (from high to low) that the modification requires is typically a critical factor in user adoption. The more that people have to alter their work habits to perform the newly mobilized process, the more they will need help adjusting to the new process, be it through training, awareness raising, or other change management activities.

## Comparing Mobility Solutions

To illustrate this approach, we compare two typical mobility projects along each of the four dimensions:

- Providing mobile email and PIM capabilities to the workforce

- Implementing mobile field force automation (FFA) in a field service organization that provides installation, repair, and warranty services for products in the field

### *Technology Invasiveness*

In the case of a mobile email and PIM solution, the degree of technology invasiveness is so low that it is almost non-existent. Most mobile email and PIM products are basically plug-and-play solutions that require little customization to provide access to the corporate email infrastructure.

With a mobile FFA solution, the story is entirely different. A typical field force process spans administrative boundaries and exchanges information with a multitude of corporate systems: CRM, billing and invoicing, workforce management, dispatch, parts inventory, logistics, and so on. A successful mobile FFA solution requires integrating these systems, which also implies developing, integrating, and testing related connectors and adapters. In addition, when information is exchanged across company boundaries, significant integration issues arise—information has to be extracted, processed, and routed not just internally but externally as well. With a solution like this, the degree of technology invasiveness is very high.

### Expected Benefits

A mobile email and PIM solution provides significant incremental benefits by allowing connectivity to email outside of the traditional workplace. The main benefit is improved response time, especially to urgent matters.

In a mobile FFA solution, one incremental benefit is improved productivity through the elimination of a paper-based process. However, such a solution can also provide process transformation benefits: improving customer satisfaction by mobilizing scheduling, dispatch, and billing systems, and reducing the repair-to-cash cycle time by charging the customer on-site for work performed.

### Solution Reach

Mobilizing a horizontal capability such as email and PIM, which potentially touches all employees, has a greater reach than a vertical capability like mobile FFA, which only affects a limited group of field force workers.

### Degree of Process/People Change

A mobile email and PIM solution is a natural extension of the desktop computer email paradigm. It does not require much training or change in work habits. In contrast, a mobile FFA solution, which replaces a paper-based field process with a mobile technology-enabled process, would require training individual field technicians in the new process and technologies.

### *A Graphical Comparison*

When mapped onto the framework for comparison, the differences between these two solutions become obvious. Figure 30 shows how the mobile email and PIM solution falls on each dimension. This solution has incremental benefits, which need to be understood in the context of the solution's reach: it is available to any employee with a relatively new phone and a compatible plan with a mobile carrier. But it is also minimally invasive in terms of technology and requires little or no training or process changes.

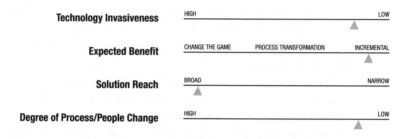

Figure 30. Mapping a mobile email and PIM solution.

The mobile FFA solution, on the other hand, affects a small portion of the total workforce, but this part of the workforce is in frequent and high-impact interaction with customers (Figure 31). The solution's benefits include some operational excellence elements, but it is more about transforming the field service process. The change-the-game benefits include using the field service organization to gain a competitive edge through enhanced customer service. But the risks that need to be managed—technology integration and process and people change—are equally high.

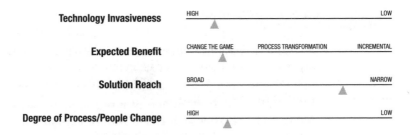

Figure 31. Mapping a mobile FFA solution.

Which solution should be chosen to compete for funding with non-mobility solutions? The answer depends on the needs and direction of the organization. The most important thing is that having a good mix of both types of solutions in the mobility portfolio leads to better overall business benefits. Leaning too heavily on any one type could negatively affect the organization's competitiveness. For example, if an organization were to fund a large number of incremental projects (like mobile email and PIM), it could discover that its competitors invested in some (albeit risky) change-the-game mobility solutions and leapfrogged in the market.

The advantage of evaluating mobility solutions using the approach outlined in this chapter is that it helps organizations choose the right mix of solutions to push for approval and funding.

# Things to Consider

- Because mobility business cases are usually evaluated against non-mobility business cases, remember to develop compelling arguments that will help differentiate your cases from non-mobility cases.

- Make sure that your business case distinguishes between quantitative and qualitative benefits.

- Business owners and shareholders must understand and accept the cross-organizational and cross-process impacts of mobility. Can you clearly explain how the benefit will be shared across organizational boundaries and how the respective business units will share the investment?

- Test the magnitude of the improvements you are forecasting in your business case. For example, does the projected 40% improvement in field force productivity really stand up to industry experience?

- Use scenarios to test the validity of the business case against variations in the key benefits and improvements. Usually three scenarios—worst, likely, and best—provide good insight.

- If possible, use a controlled pilot or proof-of-concept to validate your baseline business case. This provides an opportunity to update your business case before you propose rolling the solution out to the entire organization.

# 11

# Getting Started

*I see mobility as the next major productivity booster for large organizations—like e-business in the late 1990s. But as with e-business, reaping the benefits of mobility requires a gradual transformation that takes into account your entire business. And you have to maintain the right balance between technology, business model, and end-user behavior.*

—*Mikko Kosonen, CIO and Senior VP*
*Nokia Business Infrastructure*

As we have emphasized throughout this book, embedding mobility in the fabric of a business involves changes in the definitions of and the relationships between work, worker, and workplace. At Nokia, we continue to devote a lot of time and energy to updating our people management, workplace processes, and technology infrastructure. This balanced ongoing process, or evolution, is helping us form the core of a sustainable mobile business (Figure 32).

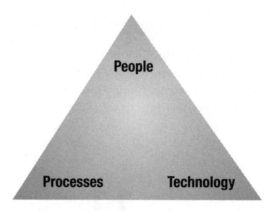

Figure 32. A mobilized business balances people, processes, and technology.

Reflecting Nokia's belief that mobility is much more than technology, we have presented a holistic, cross-functional approach to mobilizing business in this book. The approach takes into consideration people, processes, and technology—concepts that we have positioned within the context of mobility throughout the book—and how they relate to each other. This approach has fundamentally shaped Nokia's own mobility strategy. The result is our mobility master plan. A simplified version of the plan is shown in Figure 33.

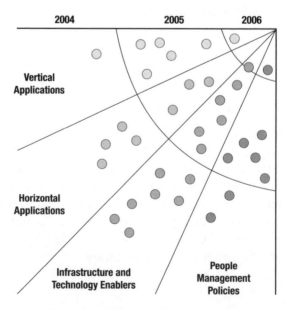

Figure 33. Nokia's mobility master plan.

This master plan guides Nokia's mobility team in its activities across the organization. Each bubble represents a function that enables a mobile business capability. This means that no function is included in the master plan unless it directly or indirectly enables a mobile business capability. This ensures that the mobility team's activities—and more importantly, Nokia's investments—correspond as directly as possible to business needs.

Additionally, the location of each bubble implies dependence and prioritization. Functions that depend on having certain mobile capabilities in place are located more to the top right. For example, the mobility team determined that several infrastructure and technology enablers would have to be implemented in 2004 before they could begin developing and implementing multiple vertical applications in 2005. So, the team focused on putting those foundational enablers in place. They also developed people management policies, implemented a few key horizontal applications, and pushed one vertical application.

As more foundational enablers and policies are put into place at Nokia, the mobility master plan calls for more focus on horizontal and vertical applications—while always keeping in mind the holistic view of mobility. That holistic view shows that mobility is really a large set of solutions:

- Business process mobility

- Mobilized company services

- Collaboration solutions

- Personal productivity solutions

- Cost-efficient voice solutions

- Manageable device platforms

- Secure connectivity platform

Taken together, these solutions help Nokia's employees work smarter to achieve competitiveness, speed, productivity, and direct cost savings.

# Stages of Mobility Evolution

Based on our experience at Nokia, both in mobilizing our business and in assisting customers with similar initiatives, we believe that successful mobilization is an evolution of capabilities—a sequence of activities resulting in increasing levels of mobilization within an organization (Figure 34).

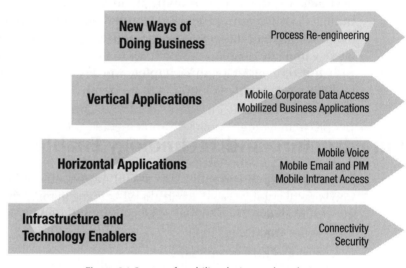

Figure 34 Stages of mobility design and evolution.

While a sequenced approach is necessary for a successfully executed mobility strategy, it does not mean that all solutions in a prior stage must be completed before an organization can move on to the next stage. Rather, other mobility focus areas can be developed in parallel as long as key foundational steps or areas of dependency are completed first. That is why dependency and timing are such critical elements in the placement of functions (bubbles) in Nokia's mobility master plan.

The fact is that, at any given time, most organizations will have concurrent initiatives that fall into different stages. For example, developing a corporate-wide WLAN infrastructure, which falls in the infrastructure and technology enablers stage, could easily happen in parallel with a project to enable mobile email and PIM capabilities—two horizontal applications.

We recommend building a foundation of infrastructure and technology enablers while balancing a few quick wins (applications that can be mobilized with minimal investment) with solutions that support the evolution to a versatile mobilized business. Horizontal applications (like mobile email and mobile intranet access) and vertical applications (like mobile corporate data access) can be identified, prioritized, and implemented according to an organization's business needs. As mobility itself matures and becomes a normal way of doing business, organizations should begin to look for ways to develop new mobility-driven applications that will help their business become more agile and approach zero-latency in its processes.

In the remainder of this chapter, we discuss these stages of mobility design and evolution in more depth.

# Infrastructure and Technology Enablers

This stage puts in place the core technological and architectural components of a mobility infrastructure—the building blocks that are common across all mobile applications and that are provided in a standard, uniform manner to the entire organization.

These components typically include the technologies that provide secure, mobile connectivity to an organization's information assets. They usually build on the organization's existing wired network and security infrastructure by providing an additional layer of support for a wireless environment. Examples of some fundamental initiatives include the following:

- Develop an architecture that supports secure, continuous remote access from anywhere—a universal connectivity layer.

- Provide individuals with laptops and access to a secure WLAN where feasible.

- Standardize on a set of supported mobile devices, including tiers of devices based on user profile.

- Secure corporate data (on-device and over-the-air) while maintaining the usability of the devices and associated applications.

- Develop ways to manage device lifecycle processes and solutions—from procurement and provisioning to usage and support to retirement or upgrades.

- Define a connectivity and roaming framework for mobile devices.

Infrastructure development is an ongoing activity. New technologies and capabilities constantly provide new solutions that are cheaper, more standardized, and easier to integrate with existing technology. Current examples include the following:

- Location-based services (applications that provide location-specific data to mobile devices)

- Voice-over-WLAN (routing voice functions over a wireless LAN)

- Least-cost routing (systems that automatically choose the least expensive long-distance carrier for a call)

In addition, advances in Fixed-to-Mobile Convergence will open up interesting opportunities for tying together what seem like disparate capabilities—location, presence, and context—with existing applications like email, PIM, and voice.

# Horizontal Applications

As we discussed in Chapter 6, the following horizontal mobile applications are usually available to most employees in an organization:

- Voice

- Email

- PIM

- Calendar

- Portal and intranet applications

- Asynchronous notification (such as SMS)

These applications are good mobilization candidates for two key reasons. First, they are widely used across most organizations, which increases the chances of realizing potential benefits. Even if the benefits are relatively small at the individual user level, providing them to the majority of the workforce increases their positive impact on the business. Second, mobilizing them requires little in the way of process changes or retraining users, which increases user acceptance. Not forcing users to make significant changes to the way they work (e.g., accessing mobile email is not fundamentally different from using a desktop or laptop to access email) makes it easier to embed a mobile work habit in their daily activities.

Mobilizing these applications will allow organizations to test the waters—without significant technology upgrades and disruptions—to see if they are ready to implement other or more complex mobility solutions.

# Vertical Applications

Mobilizing horizontal applications allows businesses to gain momentum and learn valuable lessons about mobility. The next logical area to explore is a set of vertical applications such as sales or field force automation and logistics. Compared to tools such as mobile email, vertical applications are driven by the mobilization needs of very well defined and often smaller user groups. They also usually involve significant technology integration, which can be risky in terms of disruption to core applications and capabilities.

However, vertical applications typically have compelling business cases with direct bearing on organizational goals like enhanced customer satisfaction and increased revenue—making them attractive for investment. In some situations, it would not make sense to hold back on a vertical project, especially if it does not depend too much on some critical piece of infrastructure that is being developed. Managing this risk intelligently is key to realizing the transforming effect of mobility.

# New Ways of Doing Business

The stage after vertical applications involves fundamentally transforming an end-to-end business process to realize maximum benefits from mobility. Such a transformation has the potential to give organizations true competitive differentiation in the market—to change the game by streamlining internal processes and redefining their interaction in the marketplace.

Activities in this stage also result in a highly evolved, real-time organization where mobility is embedded deeply in its business processes and is integrated with other capabilities (such as Web Services, location, and context). While these ways of doing business are still on the frontier of technology and have yet to hit the mainstream, there are some examples of this kind of transformation. For instance, retailers are beginning to use RFID to increase the level of collaboration with their suppliers and to dramatically improve the responsiveness of their extended supply chains. Pharmaceutical companies and their distributors are also experimenting with RFID-enabled electronic chain-of-custody capabilities in order to deal with the burgeoning problem of drug counterfeiting, especially in the United States.

*Think big, start practical.*

# First Steps

The experiences we have shared so far are precisely that: experiences shaped by Nokia's business environment and its organizational culture. As they create their mobility strategy, organizations must pay particular attention to their unique culture and needs to ensure good chances of success. That said, we recommend that organizations take the following steps as they start down the mobility path.

**Decide where mobility makes the most sense in your business.**
This step is critical to future success. Analyze the potential benefits and challenges of mobility in your situation by looking at the workforce, business processes, and technology infrastructure. Identify at a high level where mobility will give your business the edge you want.

**Get to know your workforce.**

Take the time to learn about and really understand the people that will be affected the most by mobility—your workforce. Interviews and observation are two key techniques to gaining this understanding.

**Understand mobile workplaces.**

Identify your employees' work types and work styles. Learn about the user communities that exist in your organization. Based on that information, design and implement strategies for making place perform wherever your employees are.

**Identify and assess your business's mobility opportunities.**

Identify and qualify business processes for mobilization. Conduct day-in-the-life-of (DILO) studies of workers as they carry out a business process in order to find mobility opportunities in your organization. Use the profiling technique described in Chapter 6 to develop an initial list of mobility candidates.

> Mobility means doing just what is necessary to get maximum effect with reasonable effort.

**Conduct a functional assessment of mobility opportunities.**

Gather the mobilization requirements for each mobility opportunity. Building on process and DILO models, identify the necessary mobility process changes. Define the user groups affected by each business process and determine how the proposed solution will affect them.

**Quantify the business potential.**

Does this solution create value? To get funding, the project should show quantitative and qualitative benefits, and should have mechanisms to measure them.

**Define the solution design.**

What are the building blocks of the mobility solution? With an understanding of the requirements, you can build the solution architecture, including technology, organization, and process components. Based on operational design, you can also assess the gaps in the current environment and the amount of effort required to fill them.

**Review technology options.**

This includes analyzing the current infrastructure to determine how to create a foundation for mobility. It also includes choosing the types of mobile devices that will be made available to the workforce.

**Examine current workforce management policies and practices.**

Decide how policies and practices will need to change to support more mobile modes of working. Look for ways to maintain the social aspect of work as employees move toward more virtual interaction.

**Develop a business case.**

Create a business case using final cost figures from the solution design and technology review.

**Develop and execute an implementation plan.**

After funding approval, create an implementation plan with key phases, milestones, resources, and deliverables. Activities to facilitate the change process should be included throughout each phase. Finally, execute the plan.

At Nokia, we have learned that this particular approach to developing mobility solutions ensures the greatest likelihood of success for an implementation. While organizations should always consider their own specific needs, ignoring any one aspect of this list may jeopardize the success of the overall mobility initiative. We have also learned that a holistic approach is the best way to successfully go mobile. Most of all, we have learned that mobility is not an end-state that we are trying to get to—it is a journey that creates its own reasons for continuing along the evolutionary path.

# Things to Consider

Mobility is happening, so start planning for it today. More than likely, your competitors are!

Know thyself—understand your organization's readiness or maturity for mobility.

- Is your organization typically an early adopter of new technologies? Is technology viewed as a critical tool for innovation and competitive differentiation? Or are only mainstream, mature technologies adopted by your organization?
- Is your organization's culture one in which top-down mandates are successfully implemented? Or are the most successful programs in your organization characterized by a bottom-up (grassroots) consensus-building approach?
- Do not forget your users. If they are not with you, you will fail.
- Team up with your IT organization early and hold that team together. If you do not, you risk overlooking key technology implications.

Try to follow an evolutionary approach for your mobility program (enablers first, followed by horizontal applications, and then vertical applications).

- However, if a vertical application has a compelling business case, review it carefully before deciding to pass it up—it might be a good way to test your ability to deploy a mobilized business process with a compelling value proposition and to generate positive momentum for the process.
- Start with the business process and use it as the core of your mobility initiative. This reduces the chance of getting fixated on the latest device or gadget fad, while ensuring focus on solving a business problem.
- Be architecturally religious, but technologically agnostic. If you define a solid foundation for your mobility solutions, you will have better flexibility to choose specific technologies and vendor solutions. Also, strong architectures reduce the risk of rip-and-replace upgrades.

# Afterword

*Does business mobility really work?* The book you are holding is evidence that it does. The virtual team that created *Work Goes Mobile* had members located in seven different time zones. We adapted our work hours to make the most of interaction across time zones, and although not originally intended, the time zone differences often allowed our work on the book to follow the sun.

We grappled with many of the challenges discussed in this book: developing effective communication and interaction in virtual situations, creating methods to make information available at the moment of need, and striving to be productive regardless of location. Mobile technologies kept us in contact and able to work where and when we needed to. Some members learned to send SMS messages for the first time in their lives; others reviewed drafts of chapters in Microsoft Word and PDF format on their mobile devices. Nokia's conferencing system provided the infrastructure to cost-effectively keep us in touch.

We worked from corporate offices, home offices, internet cafes, cars, airports, and hotels. When we did meet face to face (twice over the course of the project), most members relied heavily on mobile capabilities to continue working since they were away from their primary workplace. And just as *mobile* work does not mean *independent* work, we found that those face-to-face meetings provided exceptional value at critical moments in the book's development.

Creating this book was just one of many activities that Nokia and its employees are pursuing as we travel the path toward mobility. To give you a glimpse into how Nokia's employees are reacting to and using mobility, we took this book's oft-mentioned advice and asked them. So, in closing, we let their experiences expand your vision of a mobilized business.

# Mobility in Practice: Nokia's Workforce Speaks

### Irene Chan, Marketing, Singapore

It's great being able to get email on my mobile wherever I am—in airport lounges, traveling in a taxi, and even waiting for my kid to come out of school! There was an initial fear that work would infringe on personal time, but the reality is that with mobility, I can now manage my personal and working time more flexibly.

### Stephanie Werner, Human Resources, New York, USA

I am not an early morning person, but with my 9500 Communicator, I can easily do my first email check from home while sitting at the breakfast table. I can also answer email at odd hours, which is common in my job since I have to deal with people in so many different time zones. The great thing is, I can do all of this without a big effort to establish a network connection with my laptop. I simply open my phone and I'm connected. That's a big reason why it does not bother me to work at odd hours.

Here is something else that makes me happy about being mobile: on Fridays at the airport in Helsinki, I can quickly answer last-minute email, so that when I arrive in New York late Friday, I've already answered my email. Even if a few more have come in, I can answer them on the taxi ride home. This way I can use my time well and go happily into the weekend.

### Outi Vuorio, Mobility Research, Espoo, Finland

I'm in an off-site seminar in Rome at the moment. I received an article via mobile email today that had to be commented on by the end of business today. I definitely wanted to comment on the article before it went to press, so I opened the document on my mobile device, inserted comments directly into the document, and sent it back to the journalist. In the old days, I would not have been able to be online with my laptop all the time (if at all!) waiting for the document to arrive so I could comment on it right away. Most likely I would have missed the opportunity to comment, given that articles get published according to the paper's deadline—whether or not I comment on them.

### Donna Hahn, Workplace Resources, Texas, USA

Mobile working has definitely broadened my mindset with regard to work. For example, a powerful lesson I've learned is that work is no longer centered around where you are *physically*, but rather on the *outcome* that you produce at the end of the day. It has actually been liberating for me, since I've worked at my car dealership (they have network connections), at home, in airports, in hotel rooms, at botanical gardens, at restaurants, and at various Nokia offices. I've collaborated with different groups from several hotel rooms and even from taxis! Technology has removed constraints from the workplace and given the power to the employee. As you can tell, I'm passionate about technology and mobile working because, quite frankly, I like the options it provides and the focus on results—not office space.

### Ang SengHau, Solutions, Cyberjaya, Malaysia

A little while ago I took a week off to complete an assignment for my MBA program and ended up spending a lot of time in the library. During this period, I accessed my email and followed up on important tasks. Mobile chat also allowed discussion and decision making. I was very happy since I didn't disturb anyone else in the library while I quietly did my job, and my colleagues didn't even realize I was out of the office. I think mobile working is flexible and productive.

**Margarete Roos, Sales and Marketing, Germany**

This is one of the typical emails I receive from my 17-year-old daughter who is currently doing her 12th grade at a senior high school in Victoria, BC, Canada:

> Mom, sorry I really forgot to ask your permission for the outdoor trip this weekend. I really want to join the team in rock climbing but my house parents need your written OK by tonight. Would be great if you could send an email to Mrs. Forbes within the next few hours. Thanks a lot. Really appreciate it, was terribly busy. Love you. Mona

I am based in Germany, do a lot of traveling in Europe and the United States, and, needless to say, spend considerable time in meetings. In the past, it was sometimes difficult to respond to such urgent requests. With my Nokia 9300 and the mobile email solution I am using, it is easy to stay in touch with my daughter and to give her immediate support. (Although I sometimes wonder if the educational effect would be better if my daughter had to plan more in advance!)

**Laura Pitkänen, Human Resources, New York, USA**

Nowadays, I have already read my email, cleaned up my inbox, and replied to the most urgent messages by the time I end my one-hour commute by train and bus to the office. This flexibility is especially crucial when I'm communicating with someone in Europe who might have left for home before I reach the office in the morning. Now they get my replies during the same business day without delay. Getting news and announcements live, and being readily available on my phone anytime and anywhere, is absolutely fabulous!

### Eeva Ventä, Human Resources, Salo, Finland

Just before my trip to Mountain View, California, I activated the WLAN connection in my mobile device. I was eager to test how this cost-efficient connectivity method would work at airport hotspots during my trip. What really blew my mind was that, even during the flight, I was allowed to connect! And since the device's battery lasts much longer than my laptop battery, it made the long flight feel a lot shorter.

Another thing: I've never been a big-time surfer on the internet, but last summer I found mobile web browsing very handy, particularly for local weather forecasts in Switzerland. I also got into the habit of reading news headlines from my mobile. And even though I had promised not to work on my vacation, I was able to follow through on one open issue using my mobile push email, which really let me finally relax and get ready for a perfect vacation!

### Ville Sammalkorpi, Business Intelligence, New York, USA

At the moment, I am sitting in the waiting room of my dentist using my 9300 to write an email about my experience with mobile work. Talk about spending downtime productively! Here is one of my favorite mobile work stories: a while ago, I attended an internal training program in Shanghai for a week. Great hotel, but for some reason no one could get their network connection to work consistently—one minute it worked, the next it did not. Unlike my colleagues, who spent several hours in the evenings trying to get connected, I kept up with my email using my 9300, which worked perfectly all through the week. Really powerful stuff. The only thing that I could not do easily was send files from my hard disk, but even that worked with Bluetooth. In the past, I would never have thought that I could spend so long without a laptop's network connection and still get my work done.

### Karen Low, Marketing Communications, Singapore

My regional marketing team faces many challenges: time, environment, and geographic location. But mobile connectivity liberates us. For example, I can do net meetings with Finland even if I'm in a hotel room in Kuala Lumpur. I can connect to the office while traipsing through Port Douglas scouting new locations for customer events. It's great knowing that I can continue to be accessible and productive for internal and external folks. The only regret I sometimes have is that since my eyes and fingers are stuck on screens and keypads, I often miss the sights and activities around me.

There's another benefit to mobility for marketers like me. Inspiration (and work requests!) come at odd moments—not just when I'm at a desk in the office. For example, whether I'm discussing plans over coffee at Starbucks, seeing a nice ad execution on Orchard Road, feeling energized after dinner at home, or even just waiting in the airport lounge, I can use my trusty laptop and mobile phone to capture, share, and study ideas—even if I need to connect to the Nokia intranet in the middle of the night. We take all this for granted, but some local companies in Singapore are still using fixed communal PCs for company email and intranet! So I like the fact that Nokia is practicing what we preach to customers—mobility is not an application or a device; it's a whole lifestyle.

### Susan Peckham, Workplace Resources, New York, USA

Well, someone sent me an email on Christmas Day last year. I know this because I checked my email on Christmas Day! No one missed me when I sneaked off to the study to check my email in the lull between gift exchanging and the huge turkey dinner, but I'm sure the relief of a problem solved was obvious on my face when I got back. After that, I relaxed and enjoyed the rest of my holiday. Some people might call me dedicated, some people might call me sad, but the truth is that it's just an example of how mobility has helped us integrate our work into our normal lives to everyone's benefit. It works for me—long live mobility!

### Jeff Bailey, Workplace Resources, Southwood, UK

Once I was in Morocco, traveling between Rabat and Casablanca in a taxi. The trip takes about one and a half hours, and there wasn't much to look at. With my 9300, I was able to do email and have a real-time chat with a colleague at the Las Colinas, Texas facility. Great technology!

### Lucy Hur, Human Resources, Texas, USA

As a working mother with two young and very active children, I appreciate the ability and flexibility to work when and where I can. My job can be demanding at times, so it's quite common for me to leave the office to have dinner with my family, and after the kids are asleep, get connected to check email and do some work. It's a balancing act, but my mobile phone helps me stay organized and on top of things when I'm on the go.

### Klaus Seibold, Sales, Germany

While I am writing this, I sit in a lounge in a hotel waiting for my colleague to pick me up. I start my email client and bring myself *a jour* with email. I guess what I am telling you is that I can choose the time and location of work, and I do not want to give up this flexibility.

### Iris Landicho, Sales, the Philippines

Mobile email has done wonders for me—with the aid of Nokia's mobile device and the new mobile email solution, I can access my email anywhere. Now, I don't have carry my laptop just so I can respond promptly to queries and urgent requests from our demanding and adorable customers. With just a few taps on my Communicator, I can work like I would in the office—wherever I am. I know that our customers are happier and more satisfied because I can promptly attend to their needs. From a business standpoint, this means a lot since our customers don't have to wait until the end of the day to get answers to their questions. When you're always reachable, and you always show that you're there to assist, they'll be more than happy to do business with you. What more can I say? Our business solutions are the tools that make a difference. Show it...share it...because they'll love it!

**Angie Koong, End User Services, Hong Kong**

Over the past two years, my mobile device has gone from being just a buddy I have to being an integral extension of myself. I can't go anywhere without my phone—my address book, the time, the calendar and reminders, staying connected with important work colleagues over IM—they all allow me to manage my hectic lifestyle by helping me stay abreast of what I need and want to do. Scary? Maybe. But for me, with all the traveling that is so essential to my job, this new way of being mobile gives me back other things that I value in life!

# Glossary

**3G (Third-Generation).** A global digital system for mobile communication. 3G systems are the next version of regional mobile systems like GSM. 3G provides greater bandwidth and allows a mobile device user to access a wide variety of services, including multimedia.

**Business Infrastructure.** An integrated collection of business processes, applications, and IT platforms. In its widest sense, business infrastructure also includes operations and support. The more commonly used terms "information technology" and "information systems" refer to parts of a business infrastructure.

**CAPEX (Capital Expenditure)** An expense that is entered into an organization's fixed asset register.

**CDMA (Code Division Multiple Access).** A digital cellular technology, CDMA consistently provides better capacity for voice and data communications than other mobile systems like GSM, allowing more subscribers to connect at any given time. It is the common platform on which 3G technologies are built.

**Cellular phone (cell phone).** A mobile device primarily meant for voice communication. Mobile phone is often used interchangeably with cellular phone, but usually not vice versa, because mobile phones can use networks other than those based on cellular technology.

**CIO (Chief Information Officer).** A senior executive in charge of defining the information technology vision and direction of an organization.

**CRM (Customer Relationship Management).** A set of activities, a program, or an approach that helps a company coordinate its interactions with customers in marketing, sales, and customer service and support.

**DVB-H (Digital Video Broadcast—Handheld).** A standard for providing broadcast services (like television) to handheld mobile devices.

**DILO (Day In the Life Of).** A technique for studying and documenting a worker's daily activities, usually with the intent of understanding how a business process truly functions.

**EDGE (Enhanced Data rates for GSM Evolution).** A faster version of the GSM wireless system that delivers data at rates up to 384 Kbps on a broadband. EDGE is based on GSM and uses TDMA multiplexing technology.

**ERP (Enterprise Resource Planning).** A set of activities supported by application software that helps organizations manage product planning, parts purchasing, inventory maintenance, supplier interaction, customer service, and order tracking.

**FERC (Federal Energy Regulatory Commission).** An independent agency in the United States that regulates interstate transmission of natural gas, oil, and electricity. FERC also regulates natural gas and hydropower projects.

**FFA (Field Force Automation).** An endeavor that focuses on automating the processes and activities of an organization's field-based workforce.

**Flextime.** An arrangement by which employees set their own work schedules, but especially their starting and finishing hours. Also known as *flexitime*.

**FlexiSpace.** A concept in corporate real estate that de-emphasizes the traditional notion of an office environment for every employee. It focuses on creating flexible workspaces that support different types of work activities, including individual, small group, and large group work. With FlexiSpace, workspace is used on an as-needed basis rather than being assigned to a specific employee.

**FMC (Fixed-to-Mobile Convergence).** A technology that integrates mobile and fixed-line networks to provide voice communication services to mobile workers regardless of their location, access technology, or communication device.

**Gateway.** A device that converts information from one protocol to another. For example, a gateway would translate data formats, signaling protocols, and address information between a PSTN and an IP-based network. It would do the same between a local area network (LAN) and a wide area network (WAN).

**GPRS (General Packet Radio Service).** A mobile service that gives packet-switched access over GSM to external data networks. GPRS offers a permanent connection between a wireless device and the network.

**GPS (Global Positioning System).** A satellite-based positioning system that is used to read geographical position. It is also a source for accurate coordinated universal time (UTC).

**GSM (Global System for Mobile communications).** A digital cellular system that is the standard in Europe and Asia. GSM uses narrowband TDMA, which allows eight calls on the same radio frequency.

**Horizontal application.** A business application used by a majority of workers in an organization. Email and PIM are examples of common horizontal applications.

**IP (Internet Protocol).** A protocol that is used to send data in the form of packets across a network (such as the internet).

**IPSec (IP Security).** A set of protocols that support secure exchange of packets at the IP layer. IPSec is widely used to implement virtual private networks (VPNs).

**IT (Information Technology).** A field that focuses on the design, development, installation, and implementation of information systems and applications. In business, the organization that manages technology-related activities.

**KPI (Key Performance Indicator).** An indicator that helps an organization define and measure progress toward organizational goals. KPIs are quantifiable, agreed-upon measurements that reflect an organization's critical success factors.

**LAN (Local Area Network).** A computer network that is limited to a small area (a building or a campus).

**Laptop mobile.** A mode of work where employees are free to work away from the traditional office desk because their laptops provide the tools and access they need to accomplish their work.

**LSP (Logistics Service Provider).** An organization that offers logistics services. An LSP can provide services such as inventory control, order taking, inventory picking and packing, shipping, distribution, and reporting.

**MMC (Multimedia Memory Card).** A card used to store data for digital mobile devices such as mobile phones, cameras, PDAs, music players, and printers.

**Mobile.** Able to move or be moved easily.

**Mobile business.** An organization that has enhanced its business processes, infrastructure, tools, and culture to support dynamic, flexible, and efficient ways of getting work done. Workers in a mobile business are free from the constraints of geography and time, allowing them to move freely while sustaining and/or increasing their productivity.

**Mobile device.** A device—together with the software, applications, and content directly related to the device—that functions within and is supported by a wireless communication infrastructure. A mobile device can be, for example, a mobile phone or a PDA.

**Mobile phone.** A mobile device primarily meant for voice communication. Mobile phone is often used interchangeably with cellular phone, but mobile phones can also use networks other than those based on cellular technology.

**Mobile worker.** A worker with the ability to work where, when, and how it makes sense while maintaining his or her productivity and making beneficial contributions to the business.

**Mobility.** The state or condition of moving freely. From a business perspective, it means freedom to collaborate and transact business outside the traditional constraints of time and place.

**NFC (Near Field Communication).** A standard for short-range wireless connections. Using NFC, devices can communicate when they are within a short distance of each other.

**NPV (Net Present Value).** A financial model that analyzes the potential profit of an investment by subtracting the present value of cash outflows from the present value of cash inflows.

**OPEX (Operating Expenditure).** A set of expenses that are required to operate a business, including employee wages, telecommunications costs, real estate payments, maintenance fees, utilities, insurance, sales and marketing, training, and customer service.

**PBX (Private Branch Exchange).** A private telephone network used within a large organization. A PBX allows users to share a certain number of outside lines to make external telephone calls.

**PDA (Personal Digital Assistant).** A data-centric handheld device that may also function as a mobile phone.

**Performance-based measurement.** A system that sets clearly defined objectives to measure performance and progress toward organizational goals.

**PIM (Personal Information Management).** A software application that manages pieces of personal or business information. PIM applications usually include a contact list, a calendar, a method for taking notes, and a calculator. They may also include access to email, corporate directories, internet chat, and newsgroups.

**PSTN (Public Switched Telephone Network).** An older international telephone system based on copper wires that carries analog voice data. PSTN service is often referred to as Plain Old Telephone Service (POTS).

**RFID (Radio Frequency Identification).** A technology that uses radio frequencies to uniquely identify an object, animal, or person. RFID is increasingly being used as an alternative to barcodes because RFID tags do not require direct contact or line-of-sight for scanning. RFID uses two components: 1) an antenna with a transceiver and 2) a transponder (the actual tag). The antenna transmits a signal that activates the transponder, which transmits data back to the antenna. Retail stores often use RFID technology for clothes and other expensive goods because the tag can set off an alarm if the tagged product is taken out of the shop before being deactivated.

**Real-time access.** A method where information is updated and made available as it is received. In terms of mobility, real-time access means direct access to the most current information available.

**ROI (Return on Investment).** A method for determining whether an investment will generate acceptable returns. ROI compares the estimated gain or loss to the original investment.

**Right-time access.** A method where information is updated in less time than a business process's standard cycle, but is not updated in real time. In terms of mobility, right-time access means having access to information that is current enough to meet a mobile worker's needs.

**SAP.** A global company based in Germany that provides enterprise resource planning software, services, and solutions. The software that this company offers is also called SAP.

**SD card (SecureDigital memory card).** A small, highly secure flash memory card that can be used in digital music players, mobile phones, handheld PCs, digital cameras, digital video camcorders, smart phones, car navigation systems, and electronic books.

**SFA (Sales Force Automation).** An approach to automating common sales tasks using software and other technologies.

**SIM (Subscriber Identity Module).** A logical application that runs on a UICC smartcard. The terms UICC and SIM are often used interchangeably. However, UICC refers to the physical card, while SIM refers to an application that stores GSM user subscription information, including the key that identifies a mobile phone service subscriber, user preferences, and text messages.

**SLA (Service Level Agreement).** An agreement between a customer and an organization that defines the type of service to be provided, definitions of acceptable service levels, criteria for measuring whether the service levels are being met, and responsibilities for both parties.

**Slack.** A period of downtime, or time spent waiting. In a business process, slack time refers to time when no value-adding activity is taking place.

**SMS (Short Message Service).** A service for sending short text messages to mobile phones.

**SSL (Secure Sockets Layer).** A protocol that provides data encryption and user authentication for TCP connections. SSL is the standard protocol for secure interactions on the internet.

**TCO (Total Cost of Ownership).** A financial model used to analyze the direct and indirect costs of owning and using hardware and software.

**TCP (Transmission Control Protocol).** A common protocol used to transmit data over the internet and other IP-based networks. TCP facilitates making connections between two devices with network access and controls the order and flow of data sent between those devices.

**TDMA (Time Division Multiple Access).** A technology that divides radio frequencies into time slots and allocates the slots to digital calls. TDMA allows a single frequency to carry many concurrent data channels and is used by the GSM system.

**UICC (Universal Integrated Circuit Card).** A smartcard used in mobile devices that function on a GSM network. The UICC ensures the integrity and security of personal data, which is stored in the SIM application.

**UTC (Coordinated Universal Time).** A time scale that couples Greenwich Mean Time with atomic time.

**Vertical application.** A business application used by a specific, usually small, segment of an organization.

**Virtual.** A condition of not being physically present. In terms of mobility, virtual refers to working with people and teams who are not in the same location.

**Virtual team.** A group of people with common goals and complementary abilities that uses communication technologies to facilitate work and overcome the barriers of time and physical location.

**VPN (Virtual Private Network).** A private network that sends secure messages over a public network infrastructure like the internet using standard protocols.

**VoIP (Voice over Internet Protocol).** A technique that routes voice communication over the internet or any other IP-based network. The voice data flows over a general-purpose, packet-switched network instead of traditional dedicated, circuit-switched voice transmission lines—eliminating the need for physical wires.

**WAN (Wide Area Network).** A collection of LANs that uses wired or wireless technology to establish connections among the LANs.

**WCDMA (Wideband Code Division Multiple Access).** A technology for wideband digital communication. TDMA is associated with multimedia, the internet, and high data capacity applications.

**Web Services.** An open architecture that allows disparate web-based applications to work together using a set of standard internet protocols.

**Wireless.** From a mobility perspective, wireless is a condition of not being tethered to a physical connection point. It also refers to allowing two objects to interact without a physical connection.

**WLAN (Wireless Local Area Network).** A local area network that uses wireless connections to transmit information. In a WLAN, radio, microwave, or infrared links replace physical cables.

**Workplace.** Any place where people are able to perform their work tasks.

**XML (Extensible Markup Language).** A general-purpose markup language that is capable of describing many different types of data. Its primary purpose is to facilitate the sharing of data across different systems, particularly systems connected via the internet.

**Zero-latency flow.** In connection with mobile technologies, zero-latency flow allows users to act on information as soon as they receive it.

# Index

# For More Information

If you would like to learn more about how Nokia's mobility professional services group can help your organization prepare for and implement business mobility solutions, please contact the nearest Nokia office listed below:

Nokia Inc.
Mobility Professional Services
102 Corporate Park Drive
White Plains, NY 10604 USA
www.nokia.com

Americas
Tel: 1 877 997 9199
Email: mobile.business.na@nokia.com

Asia Pacific
Tel: +65 6588 3364
Email: mobile.business.apac@nokia.com

Europe, Middle East, and Africa
France +33 170 708 166
UK +44 161 601 8908
Email: mobile.business.emea@nokia.com

# About the Authors

**Michael Lattanzi**

Michael Lattanzi has spent the majority of his career in creative thought leadership roles, which contributes to his strong ability to sense trends and identify successful business paths. After joining Nokia in 2001, he led the establishment of Nokia's mobility strategy and the development of its mobility master plan. He currently works as a practice manager in Nokia's Enterprise Solutions business group, advising clients on mobility issues ranging from challenges and benefits to how they can develop their own mobility strategy.

Prior to joining Nokia, Mr. Lattanzi built world-class user experience strategy groups at Rare Medium and Scient during the transition to e-business in the late 1990s. He helped his clients recognize that a user's experience is a critical factor when developing business strategies—a breakthrough in business consulting thinking at that time.

According to Mr. Lattanzi, "The coolest thing about mobility is the sense of freedom it creates—you balance your own work and personal time." He firmly believes that mobility will progressively transform the business world in coming years, and that is why he chose to share his experience in developing mobility strategies by co-authoring *Work Goes Mobile*.

## Antti Korhonen

Antti Korhonen has had the privilege of actively participating in Nokia's mobility initiative practically from its inception. He was deeply involved in the initial vision work that precipitated Nokia's decision to develop and implement a comprehensive business mobility strategy at the beginning of the 21st century. Since then, says Mr. Korhonen, "It has been quite a journey."

Mr. Korhonen has spent eight years at Nokia, working in the Networks and Mobile Phones business groups, the head office, and the IT organization. Most recently, he has been in Singapore running a regional arm of Nokia's Mobility Office. Because he is married with two children (and has one on the way), Mr. Korhonen appreciates the flexibility that business mobility gives him: "I can balance my workload, hours, and where I work to get the most out of my work and family life."

## Vishy Gopalakrishnan

Vishy Gopalakrishnan is a practice manager in Nokia's Enterprise Solutions business group. Prior to joining Nokia, he worked at Capgemini as the mobility solutions manager for the Americas. His responsibilities included everything from defining the solution portfolio to developing alliance relationships to consulting with clients. His experience at Capgemini includes consulting with Global 1000 organizations across several industry sectors on IT strategy, IT governance, IT operations, and technology architecture. Prior to Capgemini, Vishy worked in Motorola's Cellular Infrastructure Group.

Vishy believes that *Work Goes Mobile* focuses on where mobility can take us in the next few years. "But," he adds, "we're just at the beginning of a huge transformation in the way we work, play, and live. Mobility, along with other social and technological forces, is leading that transformation."